Strategy Metrics

Simple Finance Tools for Strategic Decisions and Value Creation

World Scientific Series in Modern Finance: Advanced Topics in Finance for the Academician and Practitioner

Print ISSN: 2972-385X
Online ISSN: 2972-3868

Series Editor: Ivan E Brick (*Rutgers University, USA*)

Published:

Vol. 4 *Strategy Metrics: Simple Finance Tools for Strategic Decisions and Value Creation*
by Kosrow Dehnad & Navid Asgari

Vol. 3 *Managing Financial Institutions: An Integrated Valuation Approach*
by Michael Pagano & John Sedunov

Vol. 2 *Valuation and Financial Forecasting: A Handbook for Academics and Practitioners*
by Ben Sopranzetti & Braun Kiess

Vol. 1 *Cases in Financial Management: Applications for Financial Analysis*
edited by Ivan E Brick & Harvey Poniachek

World Scientific Series in Modern Finance:
Advanced Topics in Finance for the Academician and Practitioner
Volume 4

Strategy Metrics

Simple Finance Tools for Strategic Decisions and Value Creation

Kosrow Dehnad

Columbia University, USA & New York University, USA

Navid Asgari

Fordham University, USA

World Scientific

EW JERSEY • LONDON • SINGAPORE • BEIJING • SHANGHAI • HONG KONG • TAIPEI • CHENNAI • TOKYO

Published by

World Scientific Publishing Co. Pte. Ltd.

5 Toh Tuck Link, Singapore 596224

USA office: 27 Warren Street, Suite 401-402, Hackensack, NJ 07601

UK office: 57 Shelton Street, Covent Garden, London WC2H 9HE

Library of Congress Cataloging-in-Publication Data

Names: Dehnad, Kosrow author | Asgari, Navid author

Title: Strategy metrics : simple finance tools for strategic decisions and value creation / authors, Kosrow Dehnad, Columbia University, USA & New York University, USA, Navid Asgari, Fordham University, USA.

Description: Singapore ; Hackensack, NJ : World Scientific Publishing Co. Pte. Ltd., [2027] | Series: World Scientific series in modern finance: advanced topics in finance for the academician and practitioner, 2972-385X ; vol. 4 | Includes bibliographical references and index.

Identifiers: LCCN 2025049807 | ISBN 9789819827381 hardcover | ISBN 9789819827398 ebook | ISBN 9789819827404 ebook other

Subjects: LCSH: Business enterprises--Finance | Corporations--Finance

Classification: LCC HG4026 .D424 2027

LC record available at https://lccn.loc.gov/2025049807

British Library Cataloguing-in-Publication Data

A catalogue record for this book is available from the British Library.

For any available supplementary material, please visit
https://www.worldscientific.com/worldscibooks/10.1142/14706#t=suppl

Desk Editors: Soundararajan Raghuraman/Nicole Ong

Typeset by Stallion Press
Email: enquiries@stallionpress.com

To Maryam—my best strategic decision

—Kosrow Dehnad

To my parents, with love and gratitude

—Navid Asgari

Preface

At first glance, writing about strategy, its principles, and its application to business should not be particularly difficult. After all, many strategic ideas appear intuitive. Questions of competition, survival, and decision making are not foreign to human experience; individuals confront analogous challenges in their daily lives. Yet, this apparent simplicity often dissolves when one turns to literature. Competing theories, frameworks, and perspectives often leave practitioners without a clear, unified compass to guide their strategic thinking.

The vast body of literature on strategy has not necessarily resolved this problem. If anything, the abundance of ideas has sometimes produced opacity rather than clarity. Our objective in this book is therefore not to revolutionize the field by introducing yet another fashionable concept or managerial panacea. Nor do we believe that the existing body of research should be discarded. On the contrary, we believe that the accumulated insights of the field contain the ingredients needed to construct a coherent and practical framework for managers, provided that the right elements are carefully selected and integrated.

Over the past five decades, the field of strategy has made enormous intellectual progress, developing distinctive concepts, theories, and empirical methods. Despite these advances, however, strategy courses and textbooks often leave their audiences with limited guidance on how to apply these ideas in concrete managerial situations.

This book attempts to address that gap by adopting an overarching framework that integrates well-known accounting ratios, core principles of corporate finance, and foundational ideas from strategy. Our hope is that this intellectual fusion brings together the best of both worlds: the analytical discipline and measurement tools of finance, and the conceptual insight and intuition of strategy.

We would like to thank N.K. Chidambaran, George Hong, Nicole Ong, and Zvi Ruder for their support and encouragement throughout the development of this book. We hope that this work provides a foundation upon which further conversations, refinements, and applications can build, ultimately helping managers think more clearly and act more effectively in navigating strategic decisions.

About the Authors

Kosrow Dehnad, Ph.D., is on the faculty of Columbia University and New York University and is the Director of New York Institute and Laboratory for AI. He has held senior positions in Structuring, Risk Management, and Trading in rates and credit at Chase Manhattan Bank, Citibank, Solomon Brothers, and Samba Financial Group. He started his career on Wall Street at the computer trading firm of D.E. Shaw.

Dr. Dehnad received his B.Sc. in Mathematics with first class honors from University of Manchester and Doctorate degrees from the University of California, Berkeley, and Stanford University. He has worked at AT&T Bell Labs where he published the book *Quality Control, Robust Design, and the Taguchi Method* (1989). His latest book, *Blockchain Investor Manual: The Complete Guide to Blockchain Fundamentals, Trading and Investing*, was published in 2020.

Navid Asgari, Ph.D., is Associate Professor of Strategy and Grose Family Endowed Chair in Business at the Gabelli School of Business, Fordham University in New York City. His research leverages large-scale data, artificial intelligence, and econometric modelling to examine how firms balance value creation and value capture in the face of technological change, with a particular focus on the healthcare sector. He has published widely in leading academic journals, such as *Organization Science, Strategic Management Journal*, and teaches courses on strategy, technology, and innovation management. He holds a Ph.D. from NUS Business School, National University of Singapore.

Contents

Chapter 1

Strategy and Tactics

Strategy without tactics is the slowest route to victory.
Tactics without strategy is the noise before defeat.

—Sun Tzu, *The Art of War*

The America's Cup is the most prestigious and oldest international sailing competition in the world. Its origins date back to 1851, when the schooner *America*, representing the New York Yacht Club, triumphed over 15 British yachts in a race around the Isle of Wight. This historic victory established a legacy of innovation, competition, and national pride that continues to define the event.

One of the most dramatic chapters in America's Cup history occurred during the 1995 Louis Vuitton Cup, the challenger series for the America's Cup. *Young America*, a newly designed, cutting-edge yacht created by renowned naval architect Bruce Farr, was poised to challenge New Zealand's *Black Magic*, widely regarded as the fastest yacht of the year. *Young America* featured a striking mermaid painted along its hull, symbolizing confidence and grace. Designed to balance stability, speed, and performance, the yacht was skippered by the seasoned and highly respected sailor Kevin Mahaney.

Early in the race, *Young America* demonstrated remarkable speed and agility, securing a strong position that raised hopes of victory. However, as the race progressed, the extreme demands of high-performance sailing began to take their toll. Without warning, the yacht suffered a catastrophic structural failure midship, causing the hull to crack and nearly split in two.

The damage was so severe that one side of the boat sagged visibly into the water, leaving it on the brink of sinking.

Skipper Kevin Mahaney and his crew acted with exceptional composure and quick thinking. Recognizing the imminent danger, they abandoned the race and focused on stabilizing the yacht. The race committee promptly dispatched rescue boats, and with their assistance, *Young America* was towed back to port. Thanks to the crew's swift actions, no injuries occurred, but the incident underscored the delicate balance between innovation and reliability in yacht design.

The America's Cup serves as a compelling microcosm of corporate strategy. In this analogy, the CEO embodies both the designer and the skipper of a strategic "yacht." To navigate the competitive landscape successfully, they must be deeply aware of their environment, rivals, and the capabilities of their organization. The yacht represents the company itself—its culture, systems, and employees—requiring careful calibration to balance performance, stability, and adaptability. Just as *Young America* demonstrated the perils of pushing boundaries without sufficient reinforcement, businesses face similar risks when neglecting structural integrity in pursuit of speed or innovation.

Ultimately, the lessons of the America's Cup highlight the importance of strategy, resilience, and teamwork, whether on the water or in the boardroom or executing that strategy.

This book discusses strategies for for-profit entities such as corporations and startups. It is designed primarily for practitioners who are directly involved in the process of devising, executing, and monitoring strategic plans. The central premise of the book is the recognition that strategy must be grounded in data-driven decision-making. It emphasizes the importance of quantitative measures throughout the strategic process, highlighting how metrics, analysis, and performance tracking are essential to ensuring the effectiveness of a strategy and its alignment with the company's long-term objectives.

When addressing the technical or quantitative aspects of strategy, the book offers explanations of the underlying mathematical concepts. The aim is to make these concepts accessible to a wide audience, even those without an advanced background in mathematics. While mathematical formulations, models, and proofs are referenced for clarity, the primary focus is on how these concepts can be applied in real-world scenarios. The intention is not to delve deeply into complex theoretical discussions, but rather to provide practitioners with practical tools and frameworks they can use to make informed strategic decisions.

Advancements in computing power and the widespread availability of software tools have significantly democratized access to complex analytical techniques, such as optimization algorithms. As a result, practitioners no longer need to manually solve intricate mathematical problems. However, an understanding of the underlying theory remains essential. Knowledge of theory ensures that practitioners are aware of the limitations, assumptions, and potential pitfalls associated with various methodologies. In some cases, practitioners may need to adjust or reframe problems to fit the capabilities of available tools.

The role of the CEO in shaping and overseeing the execution of a company's strategy is akin to that of a captain navigating a boat during a sailing race. The CEO's objective is to steer the company toward long-term profitability and success, adjusting to the changing competitive landscape and market dynamics. Just as a captain must stay attuned to shifting weather conditions, a CEO must remain vigilant to fluctuations in the broader economy and capital markets. These external factors can have a significant impact on the company's financial performance, requiring the CEO to stay informed and adaptable.

For companies engaged in international trade—whether through imports, exports, or cross-border investments—the CEO's awareness must extend to the global financial landscape. The impact of foreign exchange rates, geopolitical factors, and international regulatory changes can all have profound effects on profitability and competitiveness. A CEO who is attuned to these global factors is better positioned to anticipate challenges and proactively adapt the company's strategy to mitigate risks or seize new opportunities.

Much like a captain who must adjust course in response to evolving weather patterns or unforeseen obstacles, a CEO must be prepared to pivot and adjust the company's strategic direction as economic conditions or regulations shift. The ability to adapt and make informed decisions in the face of uncertainty is one of the key responsibilities of a CEO.

The first critical question to address when discussing strategy is: *What is the most important element by which the success of a strategy should be judged?* To clarify, we are focused on for-profit organizations—corporations, businesses, startups, and other entities whose primary goal is to generate profit. The straightforward answer to this question is that a successful strategy creates value for the main stakeholders of the organization. This leads to the next essential question: *Who are these stakeholders?*

To answer this, let us first consider the fundamental purpose of a for-profit organization. At its core, a for-profit entity exists to provide goods and services that fulfill specific needs or wants, and in return, it receives payment. For example, AT&T provides telecommunication services and earns revenue from customers who use those services. Pfizer manufactures and sells medicine, with individuals and healthcare systems purchasing these products. Hilton Hotels offer hospitality services, generating income from customers who stay at their properties. Similarly, ExxonMobil provides petroleum products, and when consumers fill up their gas tanks, a portion of that money flows back to ExxonMobil.

This brings us to the next logical question: *How do these companies produce goods and provide services?* To achieve this, two key types of capital are required: Human Capital and Financial Capital.

Human capital refers to the people who make the operations of the company possible. These individuals are the backbone of the business, from the technician who helps maintain the facilities to the CEO who makes high-level strategic decisions. It is the collective effort of all employees that enables the company to deliver its goods or services effectively.

However, human capital alone cannot create goods or services out of thin air. People need tools, machinery, and infrastructure to produce or provide what the business offers. For instance, AT&T requires telecommunication equipment such as cell towers, routers, and network infrastructure. Pfizer operates manufacturing plants and laboratories equipped with state-of-the-art technology where researchers work to develop and test new drugs. ExxonMobil depends on complex and expensive drilling rigs, pipelines, and refineries to extract and process oil. In short, these companies need *means of production* to turn ideas and labor into tangible goods or services.

This brings us to the second critical type of capital: *Financial Capital.* Financial capital is the funding necessary for companies to acquire the physical assets and infrastructure required to create value. Without financial resources, businesses cannot invest in the tools, machinery, or facilities needed for production. For example, AT&T must invest in telecommunications infrastructure, Pfizer must fund research and development as well as the production of drugs, and ExxonMobil requires substantial financial resources to drill for oil and refine petroleum products.

Thus, for a for-profit organization to succeed in its mission of delivering goods and services, it must harness the power of both human capital and financial capital. Human capital provides the expertise, innovation, and labor needed to run the business, while financial capital enables the acquisition of the physical assets and resources that make production possible.

Together, human and financial capital work in tandem, allowing the organization to create products or services that meet market needs and, ultimately, generate profit for its stakeholders. This profit in turn serves as the essence of business operation and is the primary metric by which the effectiveness of any strategy should be evaluated.

The source of financial capital lies in the capital markets, which will be explored in greater detail in this and subsequent chapters. For now, let us shift our focus to human capital, a resource of increasing significance as economies continue to transition toward service-oriented industries. Unlike physical capital—tangible assets such as factories, offices, laboratories, and machinery—human capital represents the skills, knowledge, and expertise that individuals bring to an organization.

One distinguishing feature of human capital is its mobility. Unlike physical assets, which are owned outright by a company, human capital "walks out of the door" at the end of each workday. Employees may choose not to return, might go on strike, or could be recruited by competitors. While machines may occasionally malfunction, they do not demand better working conditions or actively seek alternative opportunities. This inherent unpredictability makes managing human capital a vital component of corporate strategy. Companies must not only protect their key personnel but also ensure their strategic plans do not inadvertently risk the loss of critical talent.

Another fundamental characteristic of human capital is its inherent limitation in supply at any given time. Developing human capital requires considerable investment in education and training, as acquiring specialized skills is often a time-intensive process. Moreover, substitution for certain roles is highly constrained. For example, a company needing engineers with advanced circuit design expertise cannot simply replace them with lab technicians or programmers without a significant compromise in quality or performance.

Effective strategic planning must include a forward-looking evaluation of the skills and expertise the company will require, along with an assessment of the availability of those talents in the labor market. For instance, if a hospitality company plans to open a new resort or hotel, it must assess the availability of qualified personnel in the target location and devise strategies to attract and retain the workforce needed to run the operation successfully. Similarly, if a strategic plan involves launching new products, services, or technologies, it may require hiring employees with specialized skills, retraining existing staff, or, in some cases, making the difficult decision to part ways with employees whose roles have become obsolete.

Each of these actions entails costs, whether for recruitment, training, severance, or compensation. As such, it is crucial that a company ensures its strategic plan is supported by adequate financial resources or access to capital markets. Without proper planning and sufficient funding, even the most carefully designed initiatives may fail due to the inability to align human capital with organizational objectives. In this way, the interdependence of financial and human capital becomes a cornerstone of successful strategic execution.

Capital Markets

The capital market is where entities in need of funding, such as companies and governments, connect with those who have excess capital at a given time. These investors include pension funds, insurance companies, sovereign wealth funds, and retail investors. For example, insurance companies must invest the premiums they collect to ensure they have the necessary funds to compensate policyholders—such as a homeowner with insurance—when a covered event, like a hurricane, causes damage.

Investors expect a return on their investment that is commensurate with the risk involved. Suppose an investor purchases equity in a company for a year. If P_0 is the initial price paid and P_1 is the price after one year, the price return over the year is

$$(P_1 - P_0)/P_0 = P_1/P_0 - 1$$

The total return also includes any interim cash flows, such as dividends received during the investment period, which can be expressed as

$$(P_1 + \text{Cash Flow} - \text{P}_0)/P_0$$

Now comes the question of risk—how should it be measured? There are various definitions, including the probability of loss or the maximum possible loss. One widely accepted definition is the volatility of returns. This definition is particularly useful when considering returns over an extended period rather than a single time frame.

When dealing with an investment horizon spanning multiple years, one common approach is to calculate the average annual return. Suppose the investment lasts n years, with annual returns $R_1, R_2, \ldots, R_n$. The average return is $\left(\sum R_i\right)/n$. Another way to assess long-term returns is to determine the constant rate at which an initial investment of one dollar should have grown to reach its final value. In other words, we seek the Compound Annual Growth Rate (CAGR) of the investment. The CAGR represents the single annualized rate of return at which an investment would have grown if it had compounded steadily over n years. Mathematically, CAGR is defined as the rate R that satisfies

$$(1 + \text{CAGR})^n = \prod(1 + R_i) = (1 + R_1)(1 + R_2)\cdots(1 + R_n)$$

This implies that the CAGR accounts for the compounding effects of returns and provides a more accurate picture of an investment's growth trajectory over time.

Relationship between volatility and CAGR

Now, consider two investments with the same average annual return A, but different levels of volatility. Let the returns for the two investments over n years be $R_1, R_2, \ldots, R_n$ and $S_1, S_2, \ldots, S_n$ with volatilities σ_R and σ_S, respectively. Suppose the average return of the two investments are the same, while their risk is different, namely,

$$\left(\sum R_i\right)/n = \left(\sum S_i\right)/n \text{ while } \sigma_R < \sigma_S.$$

For the first investment, the CAGR R satisfies

$$(1 + R)^n = (1 + R_1)(1 + R_2)\cdots(1 + R_n)$$

and for the second investment, the CAGR S satisfies

$$(1 + S)^n = (1 + S_1)(1 + S_2)\cdots(1 + S_n)$$

Taking the natural logarithm of both sides for the first investment gives $n\,\mathrm{Log}(1 + R) = \sum \mathrm{Log}(1 + R_i)$

Using the approximation Log $(1 + x) \approx x - x^2$ for small x, we expand the above expression

$$\mathrm{Log}(1 + R) \approx \left(\sum R_i\right)/n - \left(\sum R_i^2\right)/n$$

Note that $\left(\sum R_i^2\right)/n = \sigma_R^2 + ((\sum R_i)/n)^2$

Similarly, for the second investment, we have

$$\mathrm{Log}(1 + S) \approx \left(\sum S_i\right)/n - \left(\sum S_i^2\right)/n$$

If we assume the two investments have the same average return i.e.,

$$A = \left(\sum R_i\right)/n = \left(\sum S_i\right)/n$$

Then

$$\mathrm{Log}(1 + R) \approx \mathrm{A} + \mathrm{A}^2 - \sigma_R^2 \quad \text{and}$$

$$\mathrm{Log}(1 + S) \approx \mathrm{A} + \mathrm{A}^2 - \sigma_S^2$$

Since $\sigma_R < \sigma_S$, it follows that $R > S$.

This result demonstrates that, for two investments with the same average annual return, the one with lower volatility tends to have a higher CAGR. The explanation lies in the compounding effect: higher volatility causes returns to deviate further from the average, leading to a drag on long-term growth.

Thus, while average annual return is a useful metric, it does not capture the full picture of investment performance. Volatility plays a critical role in determining the actual compounded growth of an investment over time, reinforcing why fewer volatile investments are often more desirable for long-term wealth creation.

This brings us to a fundamental concept in finance: *risk-adjusted returns*. In simple terms, this refers to how much risk we have undertaken to achieve a certain level of return. A high and attractive return may seem desirable, but we must ask ourselves—have we taken an excessive risk to achieve it? If so, we may have simply been fortunate this time, but the outcome could have easily gone the other way, leading to significant losses.

To properly evaluate an investment's return, we must adjust it for the level of risk involved. This is the essence of risk-adjusted return. As discussed earlier, standard deviation (σ) is a widely accepted measure of risk, as it quantifies the variability or volatility of returns.

Additionally, an investor always has the option of placing money in a virtually risk-free investment, such as lending to the U.S. government by purchasing Treasury securities. The return on such an investment is referred to as the risk-free rate (f). When an investor chooses to invest in a riskier asset, they expect to be compensated for taking on that additional uncertainty. The extra return earned above the risk-free rate, known as the risk premium, is calculated as

$$R - f$$

where R represents the return of the investment.

However, to truly assess whether an investment's return is justified relative to its risk, we must standardize this excess return by the investment's risk (measured by standard deviation). This leads to the concept of the Sharpe Ratio, which is defined as

$$(R - f)/\sigma$$

The Sharpe Ratio helps investors compare different investments by showing how much return is earned per unit of risk. A higher Sharpe Ratio indicates a more favorable risk-adjusted return, meaning the investment provides a better reward for the level of risk taken.

By using risk-adjusted measures like the Sharpe Ratio, investors can make more informed decisions, ensuring that they are not just chasing high returns but also considering the risks associated with their choices.

Returning to the subject of capital markets, the need for capital is a fundamental requirement for companies to operate and expand. Capital enables businesses to invest in growth, research and development, and other essential operational and strategic activities. To access this capital, companies often turn to capital markets, where they can raise the funds needed for their ventures. The capital market is a diverse and dynamic ecosystem, consisting of various participants with distinct roles and motivations.

One key group of capital market participants are the providers of capital. These are entities that currently have excess capital and seek to invest in it for future needs, generating returns along the way. Providers of capital include large institutional investors such as insurance companies, pension funds, and sovereign wealth funds.

For instance, insurance companies play a crucial role in capital markets. They collect premiums from policyholders—whether for life insurance, health insurance, or property insurance—and invest these funds to ensure that they can meet future obligations. The investments made by insurance companies are designed to grow over time, ensuring that they have sufficient reserves to cover potential future claims. These claims could arise from a range of scenarios, such as paying out death benefits to life insurance policyholders or covering damages from natural disasters like floods or hurricanes.

Similarly, pension funds also act as major capital market participants. These funds manage contributions made by employees and employers, with the objective of investing these funds to ensure that there are sufficient resources available to provide retirees with income during their retirement years. Pension funds typically have long-term investment horizons and are generally focused on stability and steady growth.

Another significant player in the global capital markets is sovereign wealth funds, such as Norway's Sovereign Wealth Fund. These funds are typically established by governments to manage national wealth accumulated from resources like oil, gas, or other natural resources. The Norwegian Sovereign Wealth Fund, for example, invests the revenue generated from the country's North Sea oil production. The goal of such funds is to ensure that, when finite resources like oil begin to deplete, the country can still support its citizens through the returns generated by these investments, ensuring long-term financial stability for the nation.

Beyond institutional investors, retail investors—individuals investing their personal savings—also play an important role in capital markets. These investors typically seek returns on their investments to fund future expenses, such as retirement.

Besides companies, other entities, such as governments, also access capital through the capital markets. For example, some governments—like that of the United States—are major borrowers in these markets, often to help fund budget deficits.

Clearly, the risk appetite of capital providers varies significantly. For instance, a retired individual is likely to pursue a conservative investment strategy, while a venture capitalist actively seeks high-risk opportunities. The latter may invest in numerous startups, expecting some to fail and others to break even, with the hope that a few will become "unicorns" and achieve massive success, like Facebook.

One of the primary roles of financial institutions is to design financial products with risk-return profiles that align with the diverse objectives of different investors.

The two primary instruments for raising capital are debt and equity, each characterized by distinct risk-return profiles. Debt typically entails fixed income securities that obligate the issuer to make periodic interest (coupon) payments and repay the principal at maturity. These obligations are contractual; failure to meet them can result in default and potentially force the issuer into bankruptcy proceedings. Importantly, debtholders do not participate in the residual profits of the firm—they are entitled only to predefined interest payments and principal repayment, regardless of the firm's financial performance.

In contrast, equity represents a residual claim on the firm's assets and earnings. Equity investors benefit from capital gains through stock price appreciation and may also receive dividends. However, dividend payments are non-contractual and are subject to the discretion of the board of directors. The board may alter or suspend dividend distributions based on the firm's financial condition and strategic priorities. Unlike debt, equity does not impose fixed obligations on the issuer, but it exposes investors to greater risk, including the potential loss of capital.

From a capital structure standpoint, debt and equity occupy opposite ends of the risk-return spectrum. This divergence is also evident in the priority of claims in the event of liquidation. As illustrated in the accompanying table, equity holders are subordinate to all other claimants, including secured and unsecured creditors, and are the last to receive any distributions from the liquidation proceeds, if any remain.

The proportionate mix of debt and equity used by a firm to finance its operations and growth is called the capital structure of the company. This mix varies significantly across firms and industries, influenced by factors such as business risk, asset tangibility, tax considerations, market conditions, and sector-specific norms. For example, firms in capital-intensive sectors like utilities or infrastructure with more stable revenue often have higher leverage ratios, while technology firms may rely more heavily on equity due to greater earnings volatility and intangible assets.

Before delving further into capital structure considerations, it is important to acknowledge the existence of hybrid financial instruments—securities that exhibit characteristics of both debt and equity. These instruments offer issuers and investors additional flexibility in managing risk, return, and capital structure dynamics.

One notable hybrid instrument is the convertible bond. A convertible bond is a type of debt security that gives the bondholder the option to convert the bond into a predetermined number of equity shares, typically at a fixed conversion ratio. Because of the embedded option to convert into equity, convertible bonds usually offer lower coupon rates relative to straight debt. From the issuer's perspective, this reduces the immediate cost of borrowing. From the investor's perspective, the convertible feature provides upside potential if the company's equity appreciates, while still offering downside protection through fixed income payments. Until conversion occurs, however, the issuer remains contractually obligated to make coupon payments and repay the principal at maturity, making the security fundamentally a debt instrument with equity-like optionality.

Another common hybrid instrument is the preferred share (or preferred stock). Preferred shares typically pay fixed dividends and have priority over common equity in the distribution of dividends and liquidation proceeds. While preferred dividends are not legally obligatory in the same manner as bond interest, many preferred shares are cumulative, meaning that missed dividend payments accumulate and must be paid in full before any dividends can be issued to common shareholders. This feature strengthens the claim of preferred shareholders without triggering bankruptcy in the event of missed payments. Thus, preferred shares occupy an intermediate position in the capital structure: they are subordinate to debt but senior to common equity, and combine features of fixed-income securities with equity-like subordination.

Instruments like convertible bonds and preferred shares illustrate the nuanced spectrum between pure debt and pure equity. These financial products can play a strategic role in optimizing a firm's capital structure, aligning funding needs with investor preferences.

An important determinant of a firm's capital structure is its position within the corporate life cycle, as illustrated in the following graph. The optimal mix of debt and equity financing evolves in tandem with the firm's development, reflecting changes in cash flow stability, asset base, access to capital markets, and investor expectations.

In the startup phase, the firm is typically characterized by high uncertainty, limited or no revenue, negative cash flows, and a lack of tangible assets that could serve as collateral. At this stage, external equity is the primary—often the only—viable source of financing, as the firm lacks the financial capacity to service debt obligations such as periodic interest payments and principal repayment. Equity capital at this stage is often provided by angel investors and venture capital (VC) firms, which are willing to assume significant risk in exchange for the potential of outsized returns upon the firm's success. VC investors typically take an active role in governance and expect high-growth trajectories to justify the risk of capital loss.

As the firm matures into the growth stage, it begins to generate consistent revenues, refine its business model, and scale operations. This increased financial stability makes the firm a candidate for a public equity offering, often executed through an Initial Public Offering (IPO). The IPO not only provides substantial capital for further expansion but also serves as a liquidity event for early investors such as VCs, who typically exit at this point, having fulfilled their role in nurturing early-stage growth. Post-IPO, the firm gains access to a broader base of institutional and retail investors and may begin to build a market reputation and credit history.

With further progression into the mature stage, the firm's earnings become more predictable, and it accumulates tangible assets and operational history—factors that improve its creditworthiness. At this point, the firm can increasingly turn to debt financing, including issuing corporate bonds or obtaining bank loans, to fund growth initiatives, finance acquisitions, or optimize its capital structure. Debt financing, when used judiciously, can enhance return on equity (ROE) through financial leverage, as will be discussed in more detail later. Additionally, firms at this stage may use debt to return capital to shareholders through share repurchase programs or to maintain or increase dividend payouts, thereby signaling financial strength and commitment to shareholder value.

A firm's access to and reliance on different forms of capital is not static, but rather dynamically aligned with its life cycle stage. Early-stage firms rely heavily on risk capital in the form of equity, while mature firms, benefiting from more stable cash flows and reduced information asymmetry, can diversify their financing sources to include a greater proportion of debt.

As a firm enters the maturity stage of its life cycle, it often encounters competitive pressures, market saturation, or technological disruption that challenge its existing business model. These external forces—such as the emergence of new entrants, shifts in consumer preferences, or the advent of innovative technologies—can erode the firm's competitive advantage and compress profit margins. In the absence of a proactive strategic response, the firm's long-term viability may be at risk, potentially leading to decline or obsolescence.

To sustain growth and preserve shareholder value in the face of such challenges, the firm must articulate and implement a transformational growth strategy. This may involve strategic realignment of core business operations, which can take several forms:

- **Business Model Innovation:** Redefining the firm's value proposition, customer segments, or revenue streams in response to shifting market dynamics. This may include transitioning from a product-centric to a service-centric model or incorporating digital platforms and ecosystems.
- **Portfolio Rationalization:** Divesting, spinning off, or discontinuing underperforming or non-core business units to sharpen strategic focus and reallocate resources to higher-growth areas. This process may involve corporate restructuring or strategic asset reconfiguration.
- **Strategic Pivoting:** Shifting the firm's emphasis toward emerging products, services, or technologies that align with future market demand. For example, a legacy manufacturing firm may pivot to smart technologies or IoT-enabled solutions to remain competitive.

- **New Business Development:** Entering new markets or launching new business lines, either organically or through mergers and acquisitions (M&A), to capture growth opportunities created by technological advancement or unmet customer needs.

The following are some examples:

IBM: From Hardware to Cognitive Computing and Cloud Services

IBM (International Business Machines Corporation), once the global leader in mainframe and enterprise hardware, faced intense competition in the late 20th and early 21st centuries from low-cost hardware manufacturers and emerging software companies. Demand for traditional hardware declined as computing became commoditized.

Strategic Transformation

- **Business Model Shift:** IBM pivoted away from low-margin hardware and redefined itself as a provider of enterprise software, IT consulting, cloud computing, and AI solutions.
- **Portfolio Rationalization:** In 2005, IBM sold its PC business to Lenovo, followed by the divestiture of its x86 server business in 2014.
- **New Capabilities:** Significant investment was made in cloud infrastructure (IBM Cloud) and cognitive computing, most notably with the development of IBM Watson, its AI platform.
- **Acquisitions:** In 2019, IBM acquired Red Hat for $34 billion to strengthen its position in the hybrid cloud market.

To support the Red Hat acquisition, IBM increased its leverage, issuing billions in debt, reflecting a strategic capital reallocation to pursue high-growth, high-margin segments.

Netflix: From DVD Rental to Global Streaming Platform and Content Creator

Netflix began in 1997 as a mail-based DVD rental service. By the early 2000s, it faced existential threats from changing consumer behavior, digital piracy, and competition from brick-and-mortar giants like Blockbuster (now defunct).

Strategic Transformation

- **Business Model Innovation:** Netflix launched online streaming in 2007, transitioning from a logistics-based physical media company to a subscription-based digital platform.
- **Content Strategy Pivot:** Recognizing that licensing content was not sustainable long-term, Netflix began producing original content (e.g., *House of Cards* in 2013), eventually becoming a vertically integrated entertainment company.
- **Global Expansion:** Netflix scaled rapidly, entering more than 190 countries, supported by significant investment in content localization and regional productions.

Netflix used debt financing aggressively to fund its original content strategy, issuing over $16 billion in high-yield bonds between 2016 and 2021. Despite negative free cash flows for years, investor confidence in its growth story kept capital markets open.

Microsoft: From Software Licensing to Cloud-First, Subscription-Based Ecosystem

By the early 2010s, Microsoft faced stagnation. Its traditional Windows + Office licensing model was under pressure from open-source software, mobile-first competitors like Apple and Google, and the shift to cloud computing.

Strategic Transformation under Satya Nadella (CEO, 2014–)

- **Cloud-Centric Pivot:** Microsoft invested heavily in Azure, now the second-largest cloud platform after AWS. Cloud became the core of its enterprise offering.
- **Business Model Shift:** Transitioned from perpetual software licenses to subscription-based models (e.g., Office 365, now Microsoft 365), creating recurring revenue streams.
- **Cultural and Structural Reforms:** Nadella reoriented Microsoft's culture toward innovation, collaboration (e.g., partnerships with Linux), and cross-platform development.

- **Strategic Acquisitions:** Acquired LinkedIn ($26.2B), GitHub ($7.5B), and Activision Blizzard ($68.7B) to expand presence across social, developer ecosystems, and gaming.

Microsoft maintained a conservative capital structure, using strong free cash flows rather than heavy debt, while increasing shareholder returns through dividends and buybacks. Its transformation was largely funded through operational reinvestment rather than leverage.

Strategic Transformation Highlights

Company	Original model	New strategic focus	Key instruments	Funding strategy
IBM	Enterprise Hardware	AI, Cloud, Hybrid IT Services	Watson, Red Hat	Divestitures, Debt-Financed Acquisitions
Netflix	DVD Rental	Streaming + Original Content	Netflix Originals	High-Yield Bonds, Equity
Microsoft	Software Licensing	Cloud, SaaS, Gaming Ecosystem	Azure, Office 365	Internal Cash Flows, Buybacks

These strategic responses often require significant capital investment and organizational change. They also demand a reassessment of the firm's capital structure, as funding innovation and transformation may necessitate accessing new sources of equity or debt, or leveraging hybrid instruments that balance flexibility and risk.

A firm's strategic plan should ultimately be oriented toward the creation of sustainable, long-term value for its capital providers—namely, equity holders and debt holders. The value creation process, however, differs in form and expectation across these two stakeholder groups due to their distinct claims on the firm's assets and cash flows.

For debt holders, value is preserved through the firm's ability to meet its contractual obligations, including the timely payment of interest (coupons) and repayment of principal at maturity. A successful corporate strategy must, at a minimum, ensure the maintenance of adequate liquidity and creditworthiness to avoid default and preserve access to the debt capital markets. This involves prudent financial management, predictable cash flows, and maintaining credit metrics that align with the firm's risk profile and debt covenants.

For equity holders, the focus is on maximizing the firm's residual value and generating superior risk-adjusted returns. This is commonly measured by key financial performance indicators such as Return on Equity (ROE) and Return on Assets (ROA):

- ROE reflects the efficiency with which the firm converts shareholder capital into net income, serving as a proxy for value creation from the equity investor's perspective.
- ROA captures the firm's ability to generate earnings from its total asset base, and is a measure of operational efficiency regardless of capital structure.

An effective strategy should aim to optimize both metrics through a combination of revenue growth, cost management, capital allocation, and asset productivity. Moreover, strategic decisions regarding capital structure, investment in innovation, market positioning, and risk management directly impact these outcomes.

This book explores various strategic and financial tools available to managers for enhancing shareholder value while ensuring financial resilience. Topics include capital budgeting, financial leverage, working capital management, and strategic resource allocation, all within the broader context of aligning corporate strategy with value-maximizing objectives.

Chapter 2

Strategy and Finance

However beautiful the strategy, you should
occasionally look at the results.

— Winston Churchill

In the winter of 1996, a computer company found itself in a dire situation as its stock price plummeted by approximately 30%. A decade earlier, the company's board of directors had made the controversial decision to oust its founder, replacing him with an executive recruited—by the founder himself—from the beverage industry. After encountering numerous setbacks and failures, this executive was eventually replaced by the company's European sales leader, who advocated for a diversified product lineup to cater to different tastes and budgets—a common approach in marketing circles. However, this strategy failed to yield the desired results, forcing the board to seek a solution from the semiconductor industry. It was during this tumultuous period that the company decided to bring back the founder as an advisor by acquiring his own company. Before long, the founder—who had been fired 12 years prior—returned to the helm of the company. Swiftly, he transformed the company's strategy by streamlining the product offerings and redirecting financial and human resources towards innovation and cutting-edge technology. The impact was remarkable, as the company began to experience rapid growth, leading to a positive response from the financial market. Eventually, the company became the first one to surpass the trillion-dollar mark, and as of the writing of this book, it stands as the most valuable company in the world. This remarkable company is none other than Apple Inc. and the visionary CEO behind its resurgence was none other than Steve Jobs, whose strategic decision to focus the finances and engineering resources of the company on innovation propelled Apple's success in groundbreaking technology and thus phenomenal growth.

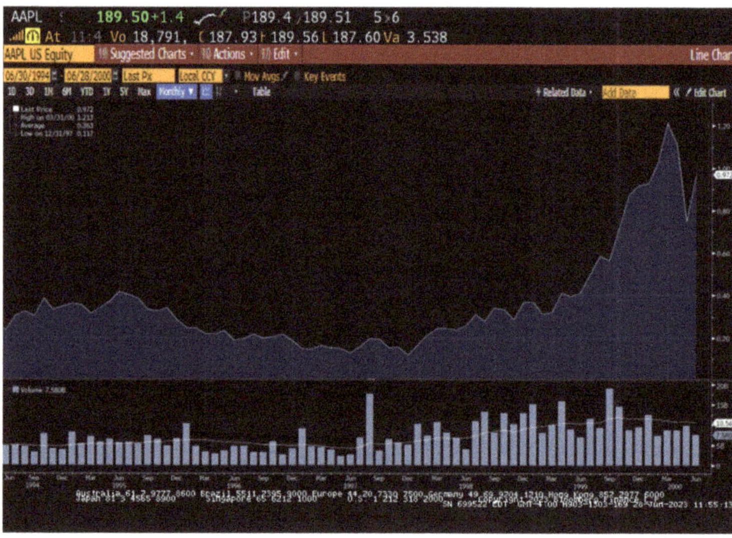

Apple's stock price trend 1994–2000.

Source: Bloomberg

During the late 1990s, while Apple Inc. was facing its own struggles and existential threats, there was another company that held a dominant position in the video distribution industry. This company operated numerous stores across cities and towns, providing customers with an extensive selection of movies and video games for rental. However, with the advent of disruptive technologies like streaming and digital content, the landscape began to change rapidly.

Unfortunately, instead of adapting its business strategy and embracing the emerging changes wholeheartedly, this company chose to stick with its traditional approach. It doubled down on expanding its physical brick-and-mortar stores, utilizing its financial resources to expand its network further. At its peak, this company boasted a massive presence, with thousands of stores scattered across the United States and various international locations.

In the early 2000s, it held the distinction of being the largest video rental chain globally, operating over 9,000 stores worldwide.

Despite the shifting industry dynamics and the emergence of new players like Netflix, this company refused to adopt a radical transformation of its business model and even declined a potential merger with Netflix. As a result, it inevitably faced the consequences of its flawed strategy. In 2010, the company was left with no choice but to file for bankruptcy, paying a hefty price for its failure to adapt to the changing market conditions. We are talking about Blockbuster Video.

Blockbuster's stock price trend 1994–2000.

Source: Bloomberg

The stories of Apple Inc. and Blockbuster Video serve as compelling examples of the importance of effective strategy. These contrasting scenarios highlight that the ultimate arbiter of a business strategy's success or failure is the market itself, as reflected in investor valuation and the market's trust and confidence in a company's management and strategic plans.

While the role of Corporate Social Responsibility (CSR) cannot be overlooked, it is imperative to underscore the foundational significance of basic financial measures, such as Return on Equity (ROE). These metrics serve as the lifeblood of a company, ensuring its sustainability and longevity in a competitive market. CSR practices reflect a company's commitment to ethical operations and its relationship with society at large. While it's commendable for firms to champion social and environmental causes through CSR, their ultimate survival and success remain anchored in their financial health. Thus, while pursuing CSR could be a moral and strategic imperative, maintaining robust financial metrics is the bedrock upon which these efforts can be sustainably built.

For instance, envisioning the construction of a new factory might appear promising within a strategic plan. However, without access to financing to fund the construction, it remains nothing more than an unrealized aspiration. Thus, the effective alignment of financial resources with strategic objectives is crucial for the successful implementation of any business strategy.

Financing and strategic planning are undeniably intertwined. When the capital market loses confidence in a company's management and its plans and cuts off the company's access to capital, it is only a matter of time before the company ceases to exist. The examples of Bed, Bath, and Beyond and Evergrande Group illustrate this point vividly. Bed, Bath, and Beyond, unable to secure short-term funding for its daily operations, was compelled to declare bankruptcy. This unfortunate outcome stemmed from the lack of faith in the company's viability and its business model and plan. Similarly, Evergrande found itself unable to refinance its debt and honor interest payments on its bonds, leading to default due to the lack of access to capital.

The interdependence between finance and strategic plans allows for the classification of strategic plans into general categories. Moreover, it is important to recognize that certain events can significantly influence a company's financial situation, potentially derailing its strategic plans. By categorizing such financial issues, it becomes possible to identify and possibly mitigate risks associated with events that could impact a company's finances, consequently affecting the successful execution of its strategic plans.

The primary goal of any corporate strategy is to create value for the investors—primarily the equity holders and lenders who have entrusted capital to the company. A well-crafted and well-executed strategy should result in a profitable and sound financial business, thereby rewarding both classes of investors.

Let's begin with the perspective of lenders—those who provide debt capital to the company. Corporate borrowing typically takes one of two forms: fixed-rate or floating-rate debt. In the case of fixed-rate lending, the lender faces two main types of risk:

1. **Market (Interest Rate) Risk:** If overall interest rates rise after the loan is made, the lender is locked into receiving a fixed coupon that may now be below current market rates. This creates an opportunity cost for the lender, as they could have earned a higher return elsewhere. This risk is called market risk, or more specifically, interest rate risk.
2. **Credit Risk:** The lender also bears the risk that the borrower might default—failing to pay interest when due or repaying the principal at maturity. To compensate for this risk, the lender charges a credit spread—an additional yield above a risk-free benchmark, typically the yield on U.S. Treasury securities with similar maturity.

The interest rate on a corporate loan or bond is typically composed of two parts:

(i) **Benchmark Rate**: This is usually the yield on a U.S. Treasury security of comparable maturity. U.S. Treasuries are considered virtually risk-free, as the U.S. government is assumed to always honor its debt.
(ii) **Credit Spread**: This reflects the borrower's specific risk profile—their likelihood of default, business outlook, and financial health at the time of borrowing.

So, the total interest rate on a corporate bond or loan is

$$\text{Corporate Interest Rate} = \text{Treasury Yield} + \text{Credit Spread}$$

While the credit spread is fixed at the time of issuance, the underlying credit quality of the borrower can change during the life of the loan or bond. If the company's financial position deteriorates, the market perceives higher risk, and its credit spread widens. Conversely, if the company performs well, its perceived risk decreases, and the credit spread narrows.

This change in risk perception affects the market price of the bond or loan. For example, if a lender needs to sell the bond before maturity, the resale price will reflect the current Treasury yield, the updated credit spread of the company at the time of sale. If the borrower is riskier now, the bond's price falls because future cash flows are discounted at a higher effective rate. On the other hand, if the borrower is healthier now, the bond's price rises, as its fixed payments are now more attractive compared to prevailing lower-risk premiums.

If a lender wishes to avoid market (interest rate) risk, one common alternative to fixed-rate lending is to extend credit using a floating interest rate. In this approach, the interest on the loan is tied to a variable benchmark rate, such as the Secured Overnight Financing Rate (SOFR) or the Prime Rate, which adjusts regularly to reflect changes in prevailing market conditions. To compensate for borrower-specific risk, a credit spread is added to the floating rate.

For example, a loan agreement might specify that the borrower pays SOFR +2%. As SOFR fluctuates with broader interest rate movements, the lender's total return adjusts accordingly, allowing them to track market rates over time. This structure provides an important benefit for the lender because it largely eliminates interest rate risk. The lender is now primarily exposed to credit risk, meaning the risk that the borrower fails to repay interest or principal. If market interest rates rise, the floating rate adjusts upward, maintaining the lender's return relative to market conditions.

In future chapters, we'll explore how interest rate derivatives, particularly interest rate swaps, can be used to transform the nature of a loan. For example, a lender (or a borrower) who initially agreed to a fixed-rate loan can enter into an interest rate swap agreement to convert that loan into an effective floating-rate loan, thereby hedging against market rate movements.

In a typical fixed-to-floating interest rate swap, the lender agrees to pay a fixed rate while receiving a floating rate tied to a benchmark such as SOFR. The effect is similar to holding a floating-rate asset, namely, if rates rise, the lender's floating-rate receipt increases, offsetting the opportunity cost of holding a fixed-rate loan. On the other hand, if rates fall, the fixed portion remains unchanged, potentially making the swap less favorable to the lender.

It's important to note that fixed-rate lending is not without its advantages. If market interest rates decline, the fixed-rate lender benefits by continuing to earn the higher contracted interest rate, which now exceeds what the market offers. In this scenario, the fixed-rate loan becomes more valuable, and the market price of the bond or loan rises, potentially allowing the lender to sell it at a premium. This asymmetry highlights the trade-off between rate stability and market sensitivity:

- Floating-rate lending protects against rising rates but offers no upside when rates fall.
- Fixed-rate lending locks in a known return but carries interest rate risk—unless it is actively hedged using tools like swaps.

The credit spread on a loan or bond compensates the lender for the risk that the borrower may default. It reflects the expected loss from lending to a risky counterparty instead of a risk-free one.

To understand this concept intuitively, consider a simple one-year investment decision involving \$1 of capital. You have two options:

Option 1: Risk-Free Investment

You can invest in a risk-free asset that offers a guaranteed annual return at a rate of i. At the end of the year, you will receive $(1 + i)$. This return is certain because the borrower (e.g., the U.S. government) is assumed to have no default risk.

Option 2: Risky Investment

Alternatively, you can lend to a risky borrower, who promises to pay you a return of $i + \Delta$, where Δ is the credit spread—the premium over the risk-free rate meant to compensate for the possibility of default. In this scenario, with probability p, the borrower defaults and you recover only a fraction R of the amount due. Your recovery is $R(1 + i + \Delta)$. With probability $1 - p$, the borrower does not default, and you receive the full payment of $1 + i + \Delta$.

To make the investment in the risky borrower equally attractive as the risk-free alternative, the expected return on the risky investment must equal the guaranteed return from the risk-free investment:

$$1 + i = pR(1 + i + \Delta) + (1 - p)(1 + i + \Delta)$$

Solving for Δ, we get

$$p(1 - R) = \Delta/(1 + i + \Delta) \text{ or } \Delta \approx p(1 - R) \rightarrow \text{ Credit Spread}$$
$$\approx \text{ Expected Loss}$$

The other key group with a direct stake in a company's performance is its equity investors—the shareholders. Unlike lenders, who prioritize security and predictable income, equity investors are focused on growth, profitability, and long-term value creation. Their return is not fixed or guaranteed; instead, it is contingent upon the company's success.

Shareholders occupy the residual position in a firm's capital structure. This means they are entitled to whatever remains after all financial obligations—such as interest payments and loan repayments—have been met. Due to this position, equity holders assume greater risk than lenders, but also stand to gain more if the company performs well.

The success of a corporate strategy is ultimately judged by the value it creates for these residual claimants. That value can be realized in two primary ways:

(i) **Dividends**: Direct cash payments distributed to shareholders from the company's profits.
(ii) **Capital Gains**: An increase in the market price of the company's shares, reflecting investor confidence in the firm's future profitability and strategic direction.

But how does the market form that confidence? It relies heavily on publicly available financial information.

Public companies are required to report their financial condition and performance on a regular basis. These reports—known collectively as the financial statements—allow investors to evaluate the company's past performance, assess its current financial health, and make informed projections about its future prospects.

By analyzing trends in revenues, costs, margins, cash flows, and asset utilization, investors determine whether the company's strategic decisions are translating into sustainable value creation. A company that consistently delivers strong financial results and shows signs of strategic foresight tends to attract investor interest, thereby increasing demand for its stock and raising its market valuation.

These financial statements—including the balance sheet, income statement, and statement of cash flows—form the foundation for such assessments and are the focus of the next chapter.

Chapter 3

Review of Accounting Concepts

Accounting is the language of business.

— Warren Buffet

The Main Objective of Corporate Strategy

Now we come to the essential question: What is the main objective of corporate strategy? At its core, the primary goal of management and its strategic decisions should be to create value for the company's investors—primarily its equity shareholders and debt holders. In return for putting their capital at risk, these investors expect an attractive return on their investment (ROI).

But value creation doesn't stop there. A sound corporate strategy must also ensure that the company's assets are being used efficiently to generate returns. This is where Return on Assets (ROA) becomes an important metric—it reflects how well management is converting the company's resources into profit.

So, how do investors and the market evaluate whether management is doing a good job? In the case of publicly traded companies, they are required to provide regular and transparent financial reports. These documents allow investors and analysts to assess both the company's performance and its overall financial health.

There are three key financial statements that form the foundation of corporate disclosure:

- **The Balance Sheet**: Typically released at the end of the fiscal year (often the calendar year), the balance sheet offers a snapshot of what the company owns (its *assets*) and what it owes (its *liabilities*) at a specific point in time. It gives a clear picture of the company's financial position.
- **The Income Statement**: Also known as the profit and loss statement, this is typically issued every quarter. It details the company's revenues and expenses during that period, showing how much it earned and how much it spent. This helps investors evaluate the company's profitability and operational performance.
- **The Statement of Cash Flows**: Since cash is the lifeblood of any organization, this report tracks the inflow and outflow of cash over a given period. It answers critical questions: How much cash has entered the business? How much is left? And from which activities—operations, investing, or financing?

Together, these statements provide a comprehensive view of how well the company is managed and whether it is on a path of sustainable value creation. For corporate strategy to be effective, it must consistently align managerial actions with long-term investor value, operational efficiency, and financial transparency.

Balance Sheet

All publicly traded companies are required to report a snapshot of their financial position, including their assets (what they own) and liabilities (what they owe). This snapshot is typically taken as of December 31, but the reporting date may vary across countries, as shown in the following table.

Common Balance Sheet Reporting Dates by Country.

Country	Typical Fiscal Year-End	Notes
United States	December 31 (most common)	Public companies file 10-K reports; companies may choose other dates.
United Kingdom	March 31	Annual accounts due 6–9 months after year-end.
Canada	December 31 (most common)	Fiscal year-end can be chosen by company; many align with calendar year.
Australia	June 30	Standard government fiscal year; reports usually due by October 31.
Japan	March 31	Common fiscal year-end; reports due within 3 months.
India	March 31	Mandated fiscal year (April 1–March 31) by Companies Act.
Germany	December 31	Most companies follow the calendar year; annual filing required.
France	December 31	Reports must be filed within 6 months of year-end.
China	December 31	Fiscal year matches tax year; filings due within 4–5 months.
Iran	March 20 (end of Persian year)	Fiscal year is March 21–March 20 (Solar Hijri calendar).

One way to report a company's assets is simply to list them all individually. However, such an unstructured approach can make it difficult to analyze and evaluate the company's financial position. To address this, the balance sheet follows a standardized format designed to enhance clarity and comparability.

Assets are grouped into categories based on how quickly they can be converted into cash. The first major category is current assets, which includes all assets expected to be converted into cash or used up within one year. Within this category, items are listed in order of liquidity—that is, how easily and quickly they can be converted into cash. For example, cash and cash equivalents appear first, followed by marketable securities, accounts receivable, inventory, and so on.

Each major class of assets is organized under a specific heading, such as current assets, non-current assets, property, plant, and equipment, and intangible assets. Companies often provide further breakdowns within these categories, listing individual line items to give investors and analysts more detailed insight into their asset composition.

For our purposes, however, we will focus primarily on the general categories of assets, as the detailed itemization is not essential to the discussions at hand.

1. Cash and Cash Equivalents: Cash and cash equivalents represent the most liquid assets on a company's balance sheet. These are funds that are readily available to meet short-term obligations or operational needs. Companies typically maintain a portion of their cash in bank accounts for day-to-day transactions such as paying employees, suppliers, and utilities.

However, when immediate use of funds is not anticipated, companies often seek to maximize the return on idle cash by investing in highly liquid, low-risk instruments. These may include:

- Treasury bills (short-term government securities),
- Money market funds,
- Commercial paper issued by financially sound corporations,
- And short-term certificates of deposit (CDs).

These instruments are considered "cash equivalents" because they can be quickly converted into cash with minimal risk of losing value. By doing so, companies can earn interest or yield on surplus cash without sacrificing liquidity.

Maintaining an appropriate balance of cash and cash equivalents is a key aspect of corporate treasury management, ensuring the company has the flexibility to cover short-term expenses while optimizing the return on unutilized funds.

2. Accounts Receivable: When a company sells a product or provides a service, it may not receive payment immediately. Instead, it often extends credit to the buyer, agreeing to be paid at a later date. This arrangement creates what is known as accounts receivable—the amount of money owed to the company by its customers for goods delivered or services rendered.

For example, consider a retail apparel store that receives jeans and dresses from a clothing manufacturer. Rather than paying upfront, the retailer may agree to pay the manufacturer in three months, once it has had time to sell the merchandise. During this period, the manufacturer records the amount owed as accounts receivable on its balance sheet.

If the manufacturer needs cash before the payment is due, it has the option to convert the receivable into cash through a process called factoring or discounting. This typically involves presenting the receivable to a bank or financial institution, which will provide immediate cash—usually at a discount. The amount the manufacturer receives depends on two main factors:

- The creditworthiness of the retailer (i.e., the likelihood they will pay on time), and
- The prevailing interest rates, which influence the discount applied to the receivable.

The key takeaway is that although accounts receivable represent pending payments, they are generally considered a liquid asset because they can be monetized relatively quickly, either through collection or by being used as collateral to raise short-term financing.

3. Inventory: Inventory refers to the physical goods that a company holds for future use—either for sale to customers or as inputs in its production process. It plays a crucial role in the operational and financial performance of a business.

For instance, a consumer electronics manufacturer may keep an inventory of components such as transistors, microchips, or motherboards, which are essential for assembling finished products like smartphones or laptops. Similarly, an apparel manufacturer might stockpile fabrics, buttons, or zippers to be used in the production of clothing.

Unlike accounts receivable, which are financial claims representing money owed to the company, inventory consists of tangible assets. This distinction is important because the liquidity of inventory—how easily it can be converted into cash—is more limited. Inventory can only be sold to parties who need or want the specific goods, either for resale or for use in their own production processes.

Moreover, certain types of inventory, particularly in technology and electronics, are prone to obsolescence. Components can become outdated rapidly as newer technologies emerge, making it harder to sell them at their original value or at all. This further reduces their liquidity compared to cash or accounts receivable.

As a result, inventory is considered a less liquid current asset, and companies must manage it carefully to avoid excess stock, storage costs, and write-downs due to depreciation or obsolescence.

4. Prepaid Expenses: Prepaid expenses are payments made by a company in advance for goods or services it will receive in the future. These payments are recorded as current assets on the balance sheet because they represent a future economic benefit—the right to receive a service or utility over time.

Common examples include:

- Insurance premiums are paid upfront for coverage on buildings, equipment, or vehicles.
- Rent paid in advance for office or factory space.
- Service contracts for equipment maintenance.

- And sometimes even life insurance policies are purchased for key executives or employees.

For instance, a company may pay an annual insurance premium for its delivery trucks. If one of those trucks is sold mid-year, the company may be entitled to a refund of the unused portion of the insurance premium, representing a partial recovery of the prepaid expense.

However, it's important to note that prepaid expenses are highly specific to the company and often non-transferable. Their value depends on the terms of the agreement and whether they can be recovered or reassigned. Because of this specificity and limited marketability, prepaid expenses are considered the least liquid category of current assets. Unlike cash, accounts receivable, or even inventory, they generally cannot be easily sold or converted into cash.

Despite their limited liquidity, prepaid expenses are important for accurately matching costs with the periods in which the related benefits are received, in accordance with the accrual basis of accounting.

Long-Term Assets: Property, Plant, and Equipment (PP&E)

Now, we turn to long-term assets, also known as non-current assets—items that a company expects to use in its operations for more than one year. A key component of this category is Property, Plant, and Equipment (PP&E), which includes buildings, land, factories, machinery, vehicles, and other physical assets used in production or service delivery.

When a company acquires a long-term asset—say, a crane for use in construction—the amount paid for the asset is recorded on the balance sheet as its historical cost, also known as book value. This figure reflects the actual purchase price and not the asset's current market value.

However, over time, most tangible assets (with the exception of land) experience wear and tear, technological obsolescence, or usage-related deterioration. To account for this, companies apply a process called depreciation, which systematically reduces the asset's book value over its useful life. Depreciation is recorded as an expense on the income statement and as a contra-asset on the balance sheet, reducing the net value of PP&E. It is typically shown in parentheses to indicate that it is a deduction from the asset's original cost.

For example:

> If a crane is purchased for $500,000 and depreciates at $50,000 per year, after one year, its net book value would appear as:
>
> Crane: $500,000
> Less: Accumulated Depreciation ($50,000)
> Net Book Value: $450,000

This depreciation does not represent a cash outflow, but rather an accounting allocation of cost over time, aligning the expense with the revenue generated by using the asset.

Depreciation methods can vary (e.g., straight-line, declining balance, or units of production), and the choice of method can impact a company's financial results and tax obligations.

Understanding long-term assets and their depreciation is crucial for evaluating a firm's capital investment, asset utilization, and long-term financial health.

Current Liabilities

In the same way that assets are grouped by liquidity, a company's obligations—the amounts it owes—are organized based on when they are due. Current liabilities represent obligations that must be settled within one year or within the company's operating cycle, whichever is longer. These short-term liabilities are listed on the balance sheet and help stakeholders assess the company's near-term financial obligations and liquidity risk.

Just as current assets are ordered by liquidity, current liabilities are generally listed in order of urgency or typical settlement timing.

Taxes Payable

This line item represents the amount of income taxes, payroll taxes, sales taxes, or other government levies that a company owes and is expected to pay within the next 12 months. These obligations arise from the company's operations and are based on laws and tax regulations in the jurisdictions where it operates.

For example, a company that generates profits in a given year must calculate its corporate income tax liability. Until the payment is made, the owed amount is recorded as "Taxes Payable" under current liabilities. This item ensures that a company's tax obligations are properly accounted for and separated from longer-term debts or deferred tax liabilities.

Taxes payable can fluctuate significantly depending on seasonality, profitability, changes in tax law, and government filing deadlines. Managing this liability is essential for maintaining regulatory compliance and avoiding penalties or interest.

Accounts Payable

Accounts payable represent the amount a company owes to its suppliers or vendors for goods and services that have been purchased on credit. It is essentially the mirror image of accounts receivable. While accounts receivable reflect money owed to the company, accounts payable reflect money the company owes to others.

For example, consider a retail store that receives a shipment of apparel—jeans, shirts, and dresses—from a clothing manufacturer. Instead of paying the manufacturer immediately, the retailer agrees to settle the payment within a specified credit period, say, 90 days. Until that payment is made, the amount owed is recorded as accounts payable on the retailer's balance sheet.

Accounts payable is a key component of a company's working capital management that will be discussed later in greater detail as part of a strategic plan.

Properly managing this account allows companies to:

- Preserve cash by taking advantage of credit terms.
- Maintain good relationships with suppliers.
- Optimize short-term liquidity.

From a financial reporting perspective, accounts payable are categorized under current liabilities, since these obligations are expected to be paid within a year. Companies must manage this liability carefully to avoid late payment penalties, supply disruptions, or damage to credit reputation.

Moreover, trends in accounts payable—whether it's increasing or decreasing—can offer insights into a company's cash flow position, supplier relationships, and operational efficiency.

Short-Term Borrowings

To manage their daily operations and meet short-term financing needs, companies often rely on short-term borrowings. These are financial obligations that are expected to be repaid within one year, and as such, they are classified under current liabilities on the balance sheet.

Two common forms of short-term borrowing are:

(i) **Commercial Paper (CP):** Commercial paper is an unsecured, short-term debt instrument issued by corporations to raise funds for immediate expenses such as payroll, inventory purchases, or other working capital needs. Typically issued in large denominations and with maturities ranging from a few days to a few months, CP is favored by companies with strong credit ratings because it allows them to access funds at relatively low interest rates without the need for collateral.

(ii) **Revolving Credit Facilities (Revolvers):** A revolver is a pre-approved line of credit that a company can draw upon as needed, up to a certain limit, usually arranged with a commercial bank. It works much like a credit card for corporations, offering flexible access to funds for short-term cash flow management. As the company repays the borrowed amount, the credit becomes available again. Revolvers provide a financial cushion for unforeseen expenses or temporary shortfalls in cash flow.

Effective use of short-term borrowings enables companies to maintain liquidity, smooth operational fluctuations, and respond to immediate funding requirements without resorting to more costly or restrictive forms of financing. However, reliance on short-term debt must be managed carefully, as excessive short-term borrowing can increase financial risk, especially in periods of rising interest rates or tightening credit conditions.

Accrued Expenses

Accrued expenses, also known as accrued liabilities, represent obligations for expenses that a company has incurred but not yet paid by the end of the accounting period. These are costs that accumulate over time and are recorded in the books before actual payment is made.

Common examples of accrued liabilities include:

- Wages and salaries payable—compensation owed to employees for work already performed.
- Interest payable—interest on loans or bonds that has accrued but is not yet due.
- Utilities and rent—services consumed or space used but not yet billed.

Accrued expenses are classified as current liabilities because they typically come due within one year. Recognizing these liabilities in the appropriate accounting period is crucial for adhering to the matching principle in accounting, which ensures that expenses are recorded in the same period as the revenues they help generate.

Proper management of accrued expenses allows companies to present a more accurate picture of their financial obligations and avoid understating expenses, which could lead to misleading financial statements.

As mentioned above, current assets consist of resources that are expected to be converted into cash, sold, or consumed within one year. Similarly, current liabilities are obligations that must be settled within the same one-year period. These short-term items help stakeholders assess a company's liquidity—its ability to meet near-term obligations using short-term resources.

Beyond these, the balance sheet includes long-term assets on the asset side and their corresponding counterparts—long-term liabilities and shareholders' equity—on the liabilities and equity side.

Long-Term Debt

While current liabilities focus on obligations due within a year, long-term debt encompasses the financial obligations that extend beyond one year. These debts are used to finance large, long-term investments such as infrastructure, acquisitions, or capital equipment.

Common forms of long-term debt include:

- **Corporate bonds:** Debt securities issued to investors with fixed or variable interest rates and maturities often ranging from five to thirty years.
- **Bank loans:** Structured term loans from financial institutions, often with fixed repayment schedules.
- **Lease obligations:** Long-term contractual agreements for the use of assets, especially under capital leases (or finance leases under new accounting standards).

Shareholders' Equity

Shareholders' equity, also known as owners' equity or net assets, represents the residual interest in the assets of a company after all liabilities have been deducted. In other words, it reflects what would be left for shareholders if the company were to liquidate all its assets and pay off all its debts.

It appears in the bottom section of the balance sheet, and it is a fundamental measure of a company's financial health and stability.

The key components of shareholders' equity include:

- **Common stock:** The capital raised by issuing shares to investors. This reflects the par value (or stated value) of all outstanding common shares.
- **Additional paid-in capital:** The amount received from shareholders above the par value of the shares.
- **Treasury stock:** Shares that the company has repurchased from shareholders. These are subtracted from equity, as they represent capital returned to investors.

Retained Earnings

The final major item on the liabilities side of the balance sheet is Retained Earnings. This account plays a crucial role in ensuring that the accounting equation

$$\text{Assets} = \text{Liabilities} + \text{Shareholders' Equity}$$

remains balanced. In essence, it helps reconcile the company's resources with the claims against those resources.

Retained earnings represent the cumulative profit that a company has earned over time, minus any dividends it has paid out to shareholders. Instead of distributing all profits to investors, companies often retain a portion of their earnings to reinvest in the business—funding activities such as research and development, capital improvements, or debt reduction.

For profitable and viable companies, retained earnings typically grow over time, signaling sustained profitability and a reinvestment strategy. However, it's also important to note that retained earnings can be negative, in which case they are referred to as an accumulated deficit—a sign the company has experienced more losses than profits over its life.

While retained earnings do not represent cash on hand, they are a key part of a company's equity base and a reflection of its historical ability to generate value. Analysts and investors often look at trends in retained earnings to assess a company's long-term growth potential and financial discipline, thus management ability and strategy to create shareholder value.

Income Statement

As previously noted, the balance sheet provides a snapshot of a company's financial position at a specific point in time. It shows what the company owns (assets) and what it owes (liabilities), along with the residual interest of the shareholders (equity). While valuable, this static view doesn't tell us how the company is performing over time—whether it is profitable, efficient, or creating value for its stakeholders.

To assess the company's financial performance, we turn to the income statement (also known as the profit and loss statement), which records the company's revenues, expenses, and profits over a specific period—typically a quarter or a full fiscal year.

The income statement is especially important to:

- Lenders, who want to evaluate the company's ability to generate enough income to meet interest payments and repay the principal on borrowed funds.
- Equity holders, who are interested in the company's profits that belongs to them after debt obligations are met. The profits is paid to shareholers either in the form of dividends or reinvested earnings that can increase the value of their shares.

Revenues

The income statement typically begins with revenues—also referred to as sales or top-line income—which represent the income generated from the company's core business activities, such as selling products or providing services. In some cases, companies may also report other operating income from ancillary activities. Various expenses and costs should be subtracted from revenue in order to arrive at the profitability of the firm.

Cost of Goods Sold (COGS)

The first major expense deducted from revenue on the income statement is the Cost of Goods Sold (COGS). This figure represents the direct costs associated with producing the goods or delivering the services that a company sells. These costs typically include raw materials, direct labor, and manufacturing overhead directly tied to the production process.

COGS is essential for calculating a company's gross profit, which is simply:

$$\text{Gross Profit} = \text{Revenue} - \text{Cost of Goods Sold}$$

This in turn leads to the calculation of the gross margin, a key profitability metric that measures how much of each dollar of sales the company retains after covering the cost of production. It is usually expressed as a percentage:

$$\text{Gross Margin (\%)} = [(\text{Revenue} - \text{COGS})/\text{Revenue}] \times 100$$

Gross margin is an important indicator of how efficiently a company produces its goods or delivers its services. A higher gross margin generally means the company retains more income from each sale to cover operating expenses and generate profit.

At the time of writing this book, technology companies on average enjoyed gross margins more than four times higher than those of traditional automobile manufacturers. This difference highlights the capital-light, high-margin nature of the tech business model, in contrast to the capital-intensive, lower-margin structure of the automotive industry.

This disparity in profitability helps explain why the stock prices of technology firms have historically outperformed those of car manufacturers. It also sheds light on strategic branding decisions—for example, Tesla's efforts to position itself not just as a car company, but as a technology company. By emphasizing its software, AI, and innovation capabilities, Tesla aims to be valued more like a high-margin tech firm than a traditional automaker, thereby enhancing its appeal to investors and justifying a higher market valuation.

Operating Expenses

While the COGS accounts for the direct costs involved in producing a product or delivering a service, it does not capture the full range of expenses required to run a company. Many other costs—essential to daily operations but not directly tied to production—must also be considered. These are classified as Operating Expenses (OPEX).

Operating expenses include a broad array of costs such as:

- Salaries and compensation for management, administrative staff, and support personnel.
- Research and development (R&D) efforts for product innovation and improvement.
- Marketing and advertising to promote products and build brand awareness.
- Human resources and recruiting functions.
- Legal and compliance departments that help the company navigate regulations.
- Utilities, rent, and facility maintenance for offices, factories, and warehouses.
- IT infrastructure, including software subscriptions and cybersecurity services.

These expenses are necessary for sustaining and growing the business but are not directly involved in manufacturing or delivering goods. On the income statement, operating expenses are subtracted from **gross profit** (Revenue – COGS) to calculate a key performance metric:

EBITDA—Earnings Before Interest, Taxes, Depreciation, and Amortization.

$$\text{EBITDA} = \text{Revenue} - \text{COGS} - \text{Operating Expenses}$$

Understanding and managing operating expenses is crucial for improving profitability. While high operating costs can erode margins, strategic investments in areas like R&D or marketing can also fuel long-term growth and competitive advantage.

EBITDA is widely used by analysts and investors as a measure of a company's operational performance. It focuses on the core earnings power of the business, excluding non-operating and non-cash items, such as interest payments, tax obligations, and the gradual allocation of asset costs through depreciation and amortization. This makes it especially useful for comparing companies across industries, regardless of their capital structure or tax environment.

EBITDA is a widely used financial metric among analysts, investors, and corporate managers. It serves as an indicator of a company's core operational performance, providing insight into how effectively management is utilizing the company's assets to generate earnings before the influence of financing decisions, tax environments, or non-cash accounting adjustments.

EBITDA helps isolate the firm's operating profitability by removing:

- Interest expenses, which depend on the company's capital structure (i.e., the mix of debt and equity used to finance its operations),
- Taxes, which can vary widely depending on the jurisdiction in which a company operates,
- Depreciation and amortization, which are non-cash expenses tied to accounting rules for allocating the cost of tangible and intangible assets over time.

By excluding these variables, EBITDA offers a neutral view of the company's performance—one that is unaffected by differences in financing strategy, tax treatment, or asset depreciation policies. This makes it particularly valuable for comparing companies across different industries, countries, and business models.

For example, a capital-intensive manufacturing firm and a software company may have vastly different levels of depreciation due to the nature of their assets, and different tax burdens based on location. Yet EBITDA allows for a more apples-to-apples comparison of their underlying operating efficiency and earning power.

Depreciation and Amortization

As companies use their assets in the course of producing goods and services, those assets naturally lose value over time—either due to physical wear and tear or obsolescence. This decline in value is accounted for through a process known as depreciation.

Depreciation applies to tangible fixed assets such as buildings, machinery, vehicles, and equipment. Instead of expensing the full cost of these assets in the year of purchase, companies spread that cost over the asset's useful life, reflecting a more accurate picture of the asset's gradual consumption. The idea is that each accounting period should bear a portion of the cost, since the asset is being used to generate revenue during that time.

For example, if a company purchases a $1 million machine with an expected useful life of 10 years, it might record $100,000 in depreciation expense each year. This not only aligns with accounting best practices but also acknowledges that the company should be "setting aside" funds over time to eventually replace the asset when it is no longer usable.

Amortization, on the other hand, is similar in concept but applies to intangible assets, such as patents, trademarks, or goodwill. These assets don't have a physical form but still provide value over time. Companies amortize these costs over the legal or estimated useful life of the asset. For example, a patent with a 10-year life might be amortized equally over that time span.

Both depreciation and amortization are non-cash expenses—they reduce reported earnings without representing actual cash outflows. Yet they are essential for presenting a realistic picture of the company's cost structure and asset usage.

When depreciation and amortization are subtracted from EBITDA, the result is EBIT—Earnings Before Interest and Taxes. EBIT provides a more refined view of operating income, taking into account the wearing out of physical assets and the gradual consumption of intangible ones.

$$\text{EBIT} = \text{EBITDA} - \text{Depreciation} - \text{Amortization}$$

Earnings Before Interest and Taxes (EBIT)

EBIT which is sometimes referred to as Operating Income is a key profitability metric that measures a company's core operating income after accounting for the cost of using tangible and intangible assets—via depreciation and amortization—but before deducting interest expenses and income taxes.

In simpler terms, EBIT tells us how much profit a company is generating from its operations, regardless of how it is financed (debt or equity) and independent of its tax environment. This makes EBIT a useful indicator of pure operational performance and can be used in comparing companies within the same industry and also in assessing how well a company is managing its core business before financial structure and taxes come into play. Further, EBIT serves as the foundation for calculating operating margins and interest coverage ratios (e.g., EBIT/Interest Expense).

Once EBIT is calculated, we move to the next two major deductions on the income statement:

Interest Expense: This represents the cost of servicing the company's debt obligations—loans, bonds, or other borrowed capital. Unlike depreciation or amortization, interest is a cash outflow and is influenced by both the level of debt and prevailing interest rates. Companies with higher leverage, i.e., Debt/Equity will naturally have higher interest expenses, which reduce their earnings available to equity holders.

Taxes: After interest is deducted, the resulting figure is called Earnings Before Tax (EBT). Taxes are then calculated on this amount based on the applicable corporate tax rates and adjusted for various tax credits or deductions. The result is the amount of income tax owed to the government for that period.

Net Income (Profit): After deducting interest and taxes, we arrive at Net Income, commonly referred to as the bottom line. This is the amount of profit left over for the company's shareholders. It can be Reinvested in the business (added to retained earnings) or distributed to shareholders in the form of dividends.

$$\text{Net Income} = \text{EBIT} - \text{Interest} - \text{Taxes}$$

Net income is a key measure of a company's profitability, efficiency, and value creation.

The following is a graphical representation of the topics discussed above.

Balance Sheet

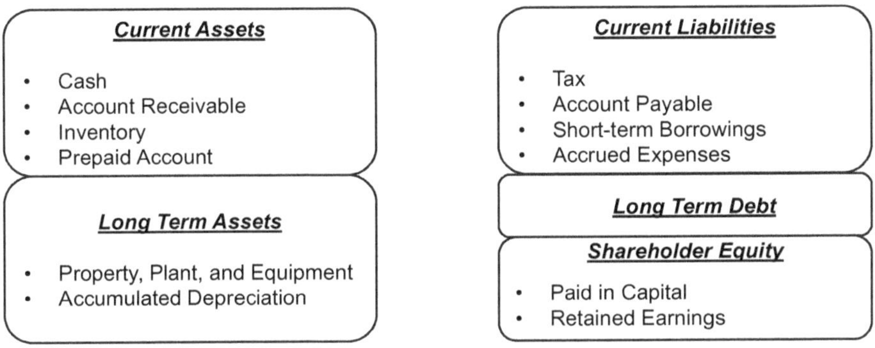

Income Statement

Sales Revenue

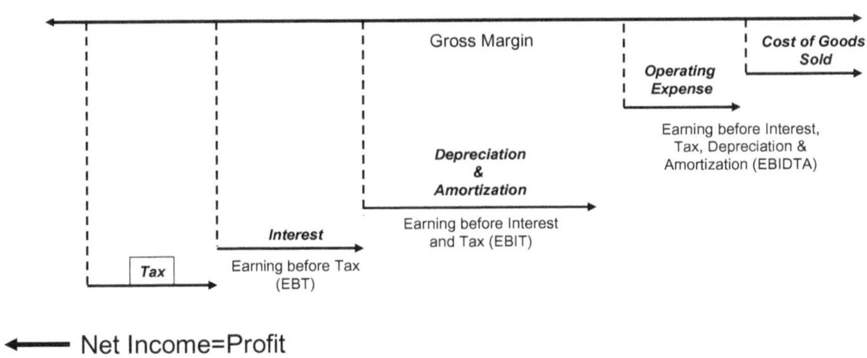

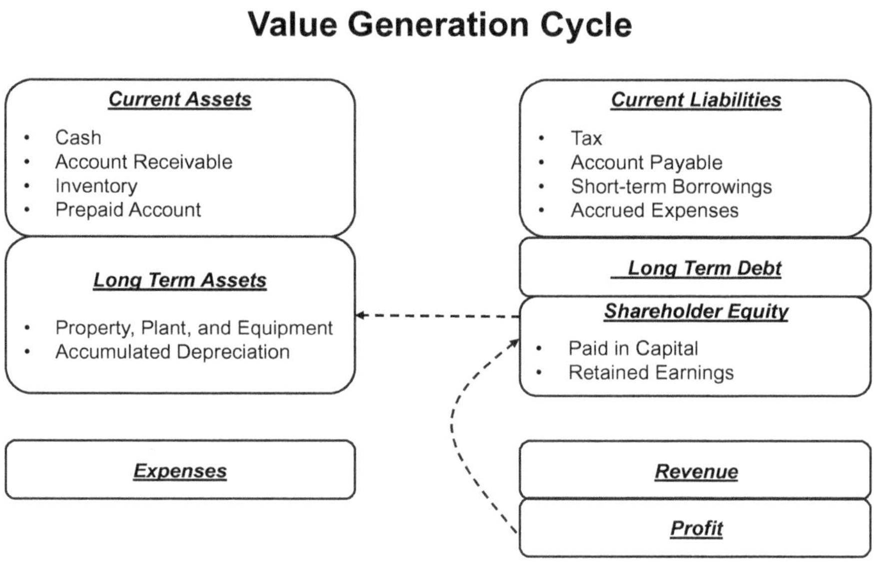

The following is a hypothetical financial statement Balance Sheet at the end of this year.

ASSETS	
Current Assets	
Cash & Cash Equivalent	$256,366
Accounts Receivable	$578,457
Inventory	$978,490
Prepaid Expenses	$117,671
Total Current Assets	**$1,930,984**
Long Term Assets	
Property, Plant & Equipment	$1,986,054
Accumulated Depreciation	($452,140)
Total Long Term Assets	$1,533,914
Total Assets	***$3,464,898***

LIABILITIES & OWNERS EQUITY	
Current Liabilities	
Income Tax Payable	$13,493
Accounts Payable	$388,438
Short Term Notes Payable	$425,000
Accrued Expenses	$188,935
Total Current Liabilities	**$1,015,866**
Long-Term Debt	
Long-Term Notes Payable	$550,000
Stockholders' Equity	
Capital Stocks	$725,000
Retained Earnings	$1,174,032
Total Liabilities	***$3,464,898***

INCOME STATEMENT FOR THE YEAR	
Sales Revenue	$6,019,040
Cost of Good Sold Expenses	$3,912,673
Gross Margin	$2,106367
Operating Expenses	$1,523,882
Operating Earnings Before Depreciation (EBITDA)	$582,485
Depreciation & Amortization	$112,297
Operating Earnings (EBIT)	$470,188
Interest Expenses	$76,650
Earning Before Income Tax	$393,538
Income Tax Expenses	$133,839
Net Income (Profit)	$259,699

A successful corporate strategy should lead to a profitable and sustainable business model. Profitability alone, however, is not sufficient—sustainability means that profits can be maintained over time, even in the face of changing market conditions. Investors rely on financial statements to assess both the performance of a company and the effectiveness of its management strategy.

Traditionally, this evaluation centers around two key reports:

(i) The Balance Sheet, which provides a snapshot of the company's assets, liabilities, and shareholders' equity at a given point in time.
(ii) The Income Statement, which outlines revenues, expenses, and net income over a period, highlighting the company's profitability.

However, there is a third, equally critical statement that investors and analysts must consider: the Statement of Cash Flows. This document offers invaluable insights into the company's liquidity—the actual inflows and outflows of cash—and ultimately its operational resilience.

Why is this important? Because cash is the lifeblood of a company. A firm might appear profitable on paper yet still face insolvency if it cannot generate or access enough cash to pay its bills, repay debt, or meet payroll. This situation, often referred to as a "cash crunch" or "cash out," can lead to default, bankruptcy, or operational disruption—even for companies that show strong earnings under traditional accounting.

It is vital to understand that financial statements are prepared using accrual accounting, which means that transactions are recorded when they are earned or incurred, not necessarily when cash is received or paid. For instance, a sale may be recognized in the income statement as revenue the moment it is made—even if the cash payment is delayed by weeks or months. As a result, a company might report strong revenue and profits while simultaneously experiencing a severe cash shortfall.

Indeed, there have been real-world cases where companies were declared profitable under accrual accounting, yet were forced into bankruptcy due to inadequate cash flow. This disconnect highlights why understanding cash flow is essential for evaluating the true financial health of a business.

The final section of this chapter focuses on the Statement of Cash Flows—a tool that explicitly shows what happened to the company's cash during the reporting period. It breaks down cash movements into operating, investing, and financing activities, providing a transparent view of how the company funds its operations, allocates capital, and meets financial obligations. Mastery of this statement is crucial for anyone seeking to assess a company's strategic strength, financial stability, and long-term viability.

The statement of cash flows can be prepared using two methods: the direct method and the indirect method. Both ultimately arrive at the same bottom-line result—net change in cash—but they differ in how they present cash flows from operating activities.

Indirect Method (Most Common)

This method is used by most companies because it's easier to prepare using accrual-based accounting systems. It starts with net income from the income statement and then adjusts it for Non-cash items (e.g., depreciation, amortization) and changes in accounts receivable, inventory, and accounts payable, as shown in the example below.

Let us consider the hypothetical income statement above and also add the balance sheet for the year before.

Balance Sheet at the end of

ASSETS

Current Assets	This year	Previous year
Cash & Cash Equivalent	$256,366	$312,039
Accounts Receivable	$578,457	$482,053
Inventory	$978,490	$827,316
Prepaid Expenses	$117,671	$92,538
Total Current Assets	$1,930,984	$1,713,946
Long Term Assets		
Property, Plant & Equipment	$1,986,054	$1,597,050
Accumulated Depreciation	($452,140)	($339,843)
Total Long Term Assets	$1,533,914	$1,257,207
Total Assets	***$3,464,898***	***$2,971,153***

LIABILITIES & OWNERS EQUITY

Current Liabilities		
Income Tax Payable	$13,493	$11,476
Accounts Payable	$388,438	$268,003
Short Term Notes Payable	$425,000	$375,000
Accrued Expenses	$188,935	$137,009
Total Current Liabilities	$1,015,866	$791,488

Long-Term Debt		
Long-Term Notes Payable	$550,000	$475,000
Stockholders Equity		
Capital Stocks	$725,000	$625,000
Retained Earnings	$1,174,032	$1,079,665
Total Liabilities	***$3,464,898***	***$2,971,153***

INCOME STATEMENT FOR THE YEAR	
Sales Revenue	$6,019,040
Cost of Good Sold Expenses	$3,912,673
Gross Margin	$2,106367
Operating Expenses	$1,523,882
Operating Earnings Before Depreciation (EBITDA)	$582,485
Depreciation & Amortization	$112,297
Operating Earnings (EBIT)	$470,188
Interest Expenses	$76,650
Earning Before Income Tax	$393,538
Income Tax Expenses	$133,839
Net Income (Profit)	$259,699

We begin with the net income of $259,699.
Next, we add non-cash items, i.e., Depreciation and Amortization of $112,297.
The next steps are the changes in the operating cycle:

Accounts Receivable increased from $482,053 to $578,457 which is a cash outflow of ($96,404).

Inventory changed from $827,316 to $978,490, which is a use of cash of ($151,174).

Prepaid Expenses changed from $92,538 to $117,671, which is a use of cash of (25,133).

Income Tax payable changed from $11,476 to $13,493, which is a cash in-flow of $2,017.

Accounts payable changed from $268,003 to $388,438, which is cash in-flow of $120,435.

Accrued Expenses changed from $137,009 to $188,935, which is a cash inflow of $51,926.

By adding all these items we arrive at $273,663, which is cash flow from Profit-Making Operations.

Next comes cash flows from investing activities, which are Purchase of Properties, Plant & Equipment. This is obtained by comparing the Long-Term assets of this year with that of last year, namely $1,597,050 and $1,986,054. This results in a use of cash of ($389,004). And the cash becomes $273,667 – $389,004 = (115,337).

Now we should consider cash flow from financing activities:

Changes in Short-Term borrowings from $375,000 to $425,000 are a cash inflow of $50,000. Long-Term borrowings increased from $475,000 to $550,000, or an increase in cash flow of $75,000. So the cash become ($115,337) + $50,000 + $75,000 = $9,663.

Capital Stock increased from $625,000 to $725,000, which is cash in flow of $100,000 and brings the cash to $109,663.

Finally, we have to subtract the dividend paid as a cash outflow. If all of the profit this year had been retained, the retained earning for this year would have been $259,699 + $1,079,665 = $1,339,364, however, some of the net income has been paid out as divided, and this amount that is a cash outflow is $1,339,364 – $1,174,032 = $165,332.

The Decrease of Increase in cash during this year is $109,663 – $165,332 = (55,669).

Direct Method (Less Common)

This method directly reports the actual cash receipts and payments from operating activities and is preferred by standard-setters like the FASB for its clarity, but less commonly used due to the extra data gathering it requires. It essentially starts with cash collected from revenues and subtracts from it cash paid to suppliers and employees and cash paid for interest and taxes, and investments.

Here is a succinct outline of the two approaches.

Feature	**Indirect Method**	**Direct Method**
Starting point	Net income	Actual cash inflows/outflows
Commonality	Most commonly used	Rarely used
Clarity for users	Less clear (requires adjustments)	More transparent
Required disclosures	Must reconcile net income to cash flow	Must still provide indirect reconciliation

Chapter 4

Financial Factors

Strategic decisions are financial decisions in disguise.

— Aswath Damodaran

As we suggested in Chapter 1, financial metrics such as return on equity (ROE) are reasonable quantitative yardstick for managers and investors to determine the effectiveness of the corporate strategy. Similarly, return on assets (ROA) is a good measure of how efficiently the management is utilizing the assets of the company. The logical next step is to explore ways in which these measures can be improved. This exploration will provide us with general directions that corporate strategists can follow. Additionally, it can help management to recognize that some objectives of a strategy may not be compatible with each other. For instance, if a strategy aims to increase revenue by introducing a new product and entering a new market and gaining market share by an extensive marketing effort, while simultaneously reducing operating expenses, these objectives may not align perfectly. It is worth noting that the specific actions required to implement a strategy are highly case-specific, contingent upon factors such as industry dynamics, competitive landscape, and unique company characteristics.

Having a general guideline is beneficial for management as it provides milestones to assess the progress and effectiveness of the strategy. It also helps identify common pitfalls that should be taken into consideration and avoided. By following these guidelines, management can ensure that the strategy remains on track and is aligned with the objective of creating sustainable shareholder value.

ROE can be broken down into several factors, each representing specific steps in value creation and capture. A sound strategy improves ROE by optimizing the combination of these factors, leading to improved ROE and shareholder value.

$$\text{Return on Equity} = (\text{Earnings/Equity})$$

This identity can be written as

$$\text{Earnings/Equity} = (\text{Earnings/Earnings Before Taxes}) \times (\text{Earnings Before Taxes/Equity})$$

(1) **Taxes:** (Earnings/Earnings Before Taxes) reflects the impact of taxes on earnings. Hence, a strategic move that reduces taxes could improve ROE. For example, as part of a corporate strategy, one approach could involve reviewing the company's legal domicile and assessing the taxes it pays for various activities. A more tax-friendly location could reduce the company's tax burden, thus improving the earnings. Carryover and tax advantages of net operating loss (NOL) are also items that can be effectively used to reduce the tax burden and enhance earnings.

NOL occurs when a company's allowable tax deductions exceed its taxable income during a specific accounting period—usually a fiscal year. In simple terms, the company has incurred more expenses than revenues, resulting in a negative taxable income. While a loss is obviously not a good thing in the short term, an NOL can provide significant tax relief in future profitable periods. It acts as a tax asset because it can be used to reduce taxable income in other years, thus lowering future tax liabilities.

There are two main ways to apply an NOL (subject to tax laws of the jurisdiction):

(i) **Carryforward:** The loss is carried forward to offset future taxable income. For example, if a company has a $1 million NOL last year and earns $600,000 in taxable income this year, it can apply the NOL and pay no taxes on that $600,000. The remaining $400,000 of NOL can be carried forward to the next year.

In the U.S. under current tax law (post-2017 Tax Cuts and Jobs Act) NOLs can be carried forward indefinitely, but they can offset only up to 80% of taxable income in any given year.

(i) **Carryback** (*Previously allowed in the U.S. under certain conditions*): Under older tax laws, companies could carry an NOL backward to prior profitable years and get a tax refund for taxes already paid. This provision is now mostly eliminated except in special cases or for specific types of taxpayers (like farmers).

NOLs improve cash flow by reducing future tax payments. They are treated as a deferred tax asset on the balance sheet. When evaluating a company, investors and analysts consider NOLs as a potential benefit to future profitability. For example, let's say a tech startup incurs $3 million in net losses during its first three years. Once it becomes profitable in year four, with $1.5 million in taxable income, it can apply the accumulated NOL and avoid paying income tax that year. In mergers and acquisitions, NOLs can be valuable tax shields, but there are rules limiting how they can be transferred.

The other factor (i.e., Earnings Before Taxes/Equity) can be further decomposed into

(Earnings Before Taxes/EBIT) × (EBIT/Equity)

(2) **Capital Structure:** The ratio (Earnings Before Taxes/EBIT) provides insight into the impact of interest payments on earnings, indicating how the company's assets are financed—whether through debt or equity or a combination of the two. This combination is called *Capital Structure* and is an important aspect of a company's financial framework. Managing the composition of debt and equity is crucial in optimizing the company's profitability. Strategies such as refinancing debt, strategically managing debt maturities, issuing convertible bonds, hedging interest rate exposure, and converting fixed-coupon bonds into floaters through interest rate swaps can all contribute to improving earnings. These topics will be discussed in detail in future chapters.

Continuing with the decomposition process, we can write

EBIT/Equity as (EBIT/EBITDA) × (EBITDA/Equity)

(3) **Depreciation and Amortization:** (EBIT/EBITDA) reflects Depreciation and Amortization. This aspect is especially significant for companies that possess tangible assets subject to depreciation and those with substantial intangible assets such as “goodwill." It holds particular relevance for companies engaged in activities like mergers and acquisitions and consolidating multiple entities.

$$\text{Let us write (EBITDA/Equity) as (EBITDA/Gross Profit)} \times \text{(Gross Profit/Equity)}$$

(4) **Operating Expenses:** The ratio of EBITDA (Earnings Before Interest, Taxes, Depreciation, and Amortization) to Gross Profit provides insights into the impact of operating expenses on a company’s profitability. While devising a strategy, managers can check how their actions may shape this ratio. Several actions may optimize this ratio, including workforce adjustments (e.g., layoffs or hiring employees with different skill sets), exploring relocation of manufacturing and R&D activities, and outsourcing alternatives. It is worth emphasizing that each component of this ratio is highly specific to the individual company and its industry and sector. It also shows the ability of the management to generate revenue using the resources of the company.

Continuing this way, let us write (Gross Profit/Equity) as

$$\text{(Gross Profit/Revenue)} \times \text{(Revenue/Equity)}$$

(5) **Gross Margin:** (Gross Profit/Revenue) or gross margin is the profit margin of the goods and services that a company sells to its customers. A higher profit margin indicates the attractiveness of the company’s products and services. However, it’s important to note that a high profit margin can also attract competition. Maintaining a consistent profit margin demonstrates a competitive advantage and barriers to entry that protect the company from new entrants seeking to reduce profitability in the market.

$$\text{Similarly, (Revenue/Equity)} = \text{(Revenue/Assets)} \times \text{(Assets/Equity)}$$

(6) **Efficient Uses of Company's Assets and Resources:** The ratio of Revenue to Assets serves as a measure of the management's efficiency and effectiveness in leveraging the company's resources and assets to produce sought-after goods and services in the market.

Finally, (Assets/Equity) = (Equity + Debt)/Equity = (1+ Debt/Equity)

$$= (1+ \text{Financial Leverage})$$

Therefore, we have broken down ROE into several ratios:

$$\text{ROE} = \text{Earnings/Equity} = \frac{\text{EBT}}{\text{EBIT}} \times \frac{\text{EBIT}}{\text{EBITDA}} \times \frac{\text{EBITDA}}{\text{Gross profit}}$$

$$\times \frac{\text{Gross profit}}{\text{Revenue}} \times \frac{\text{Revenue}}{\text{Assets}} \times \frac{\text{Assets}}{\text{Equity}}$$

(7) **Financial Leverage:** In the above formula Assets/Equity can be written as

$$(\text{Equity} + \text{Debt})/\text{Equity} = 1 + \text{Debt/Equity}.$$

A company utilizes its assets in the production process, and the funding for these assets comes primarily from debt and equity. Each financing option has its own distinct characteristics and associated risks. Debt, while relatively cheaper and more accessible, poses higher risks for the company as it entails the obligation to make interest and principal payments. Failure to do so can expose the company to default and bankruptcy risks. Conversely, equity carries lower risks for the company as dividend payments are discretionary and determined by the board of directors. The ratio of Debt/Equity is called the Financial Leverage, and it is one measure of the riskiness of a company. Detailed discussions on this topic will be provided in later chapters. The following figure shows the expansion of ROE into the above proportions.

While devising a strategic plan, a manager can rely on the chain of these ratios and see how the elements of the strategy affect the interaction of these ratios. Subsequent chapters will delve into some common techniques that are broadly applicable to strategic plans, regardless of the company's sector or industry.

What follows is a series of concise chapters illustrating the integration of these financial factors into corporate strategy.

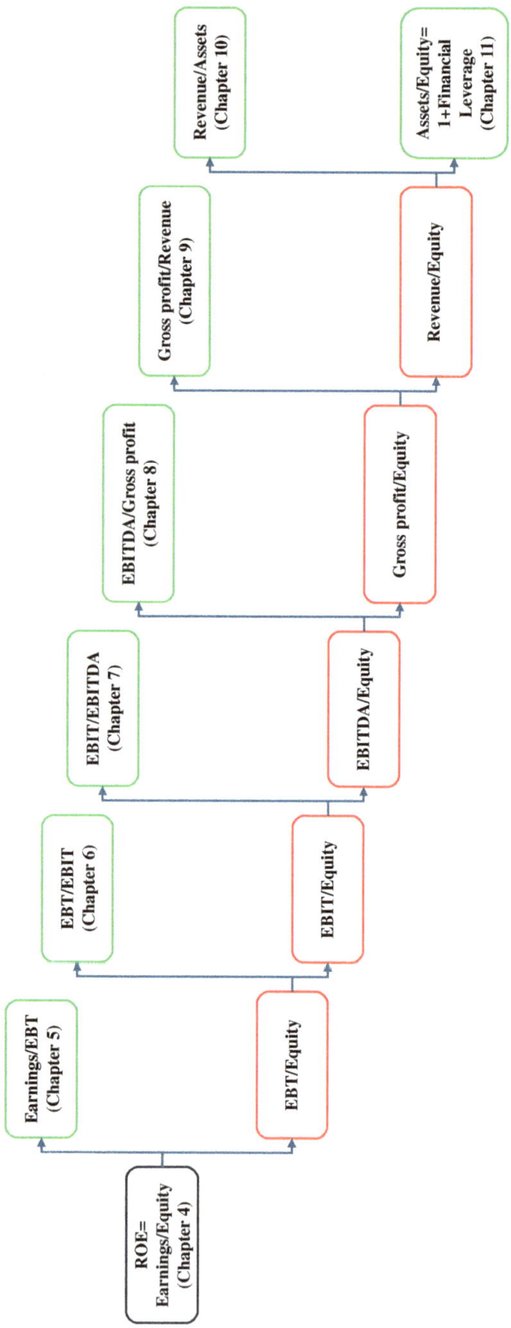

Key financial measures.

Chapter 5

Taxes

The difference between tax avoidance and
tax evasion is the thickness of a prison wall.

—Denis Healey

In this chapter, we focus on the first ratio, (Earning/EBT). Let's consider Google (a subsidiary of Alphabet Inc.), a multinational technology company that specializes in various internet-related products and services. Its primary line of business revolves around online search, advertising technologies, cloud computing, software, and hardware products. Google's profitability has been consistently robust. Its revenue primarily comes from advertising, with businesses paying for clicks or impressions on ads displayed across Google's vast network. The company's advertising prowess, coupled with its dominant position in the search market, has contributed significantly to its profitability. Additionally, Google's cloud computing services have seen substantial growth and have become an increasingly important revenue stream for the company. Its ability to monetize its vast user base and leverage its technological expertise has played a key role in Google's sustained profitability over the years. To further optimize its global tax burden, the company utilized a corporate organization that established Alphabet Inc. as its new parent company in 2015. As part of its tax strategy, Google utilized a subsidiary with tax residence in Bermuda, a jurisdiction with no corporate income tax, resulting in reduced tax liabilities.

Similarly, Medtronic, a global medical technology company, operates in various business lines, focusing on areas such as cardiac and vascular health, diabetes management, minimally invasive therapies, restorative therapies, and surgical technologies. Medtronic has consistently maintained a strong financial performance. As a leading player in the medical technology industry, the company has achieved significant revenue growth over the years. Medtronic's profitability is driven by its extensive product portfolio, global market presence, and continuous investments in research and development to drive innovation. Additionally, the company benefits from its focus on addressing critical healthcare needs, which translates into sustained demand for its products and services. In 2014, the company, based in the United States, acquired Covidien, an Irish company, and announced plans to establish its tax residence in Ireland. The move was primarily aimed at taking advantage of Ireland's lower corporate tax rate and accessing the company's offshore cash holdings without triggering substantial U.S. tax liabilities.

These cases highlight the importance of considering tax implications in corporate strategy to maximize profitability. Taxation can be likened to a stakeholder in a company's profit, much like lenders and equity investors, although it lacks influence over operational decisions. While tax authorities can conduct audits to ensure proper tax payments, they do not have decision-making power in the company's management.

Tax planning and its impact on corporate strategy extend well beyond the legal location of a firm's headquarters. Strategic decisions regarding the management of assets—particularly liquid assets—can have significant implications for after-tax profitability and shareholder value. The following example illustrates how seemingly modest tax considerations can materially affect corporate outcomes.

The first item listed under current assets on a company's balance sheet is typically "Cash and Cash Equivalents." These are highly liquid assets that can be converted into cash within one year. For cash-rich firms—such as Apple Inc. at the time of writing—the manner in which this cash is managed, and the associated tax treatment, can meaningfully influence overall financial performance.

Consider two alternative strategies for investing excess cash:

(A) Money market instruments, where interest income is taxed annually.
(B) Single-premium deferred annuities, where taxation on accrued interest is deferred until maturity.

Although both instruments may offer the same pre-tax interest rate, their after-tax outcomes differ due solely to the timing of taxation.

A Simple Illustrative Example:

Assume an investment of \$1, a constant annual interest rate of R, an investment horizon of n years, and a corporate tax rate of T.

Case A: Money Market Account (Annual Taxation)

In a money market account, interest is taxed each year. As a result, the investment effectively compounds at an after-tax rate of $(1 - T)R$. After n years, the value of the investment is: $[1 + (1 - T)R]^n$.

Case B: Single-Premium Deferred Annuity (Tax Deferred)

In a deferred annuity, interest accumulates tax-free until maturity, at which point taxes are paid on the total interest earned. The value of the investment after n years is: $1 + (1 - T)[(1 + R)^n - 1]1$.

Even though both investments earn the same pre-tax return R, the deferral of taxation in the second case leads to superior after-tax performance. This advantage grows with higher interest rates, longer investment horizons, and larger cash balances.

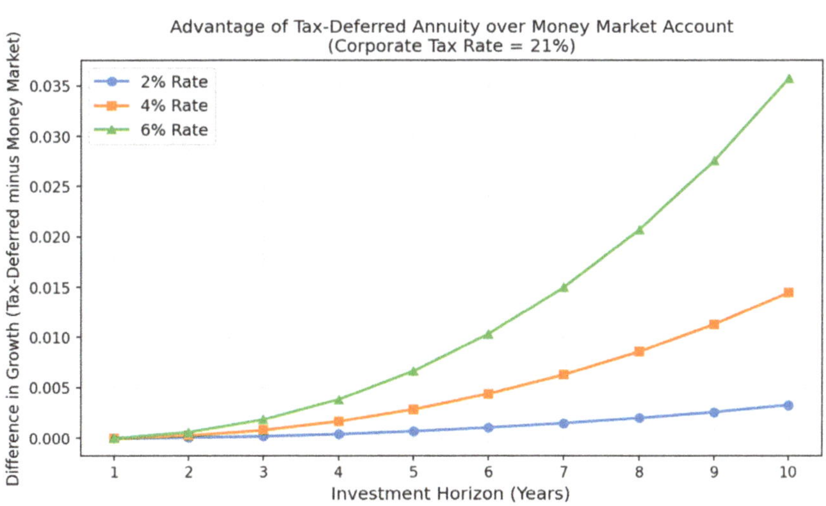

Assuming a corporate tax rate of 21%, the above graph illustrates the degree to which deferred annuities outperform money market instruments for investment horizons of up to 10 years and interest rates of 2%, 4%, and 6%.

For a company like Apple, with cash and cash equivalents on the order of $60 billion, the difference in after-tax outcomes attributable solely to tax timing can range from negligible amounts at low rates and short horizons to more than $2 billion at higher interest rates and longer horizons.

The following examples further illustrate the importance of tax strategy as an integral component of corporate strategy. Returning to the question of how a firm should deploy excess cash, one additional investment alternative is the purchase of preferred shares of other corporations. This strategy allows the investing firm to benefit from the Dividends-Received Deduction (DRD), thereby reducing the effective tax burden on income generated from these investments.

When a U.S. corporation invests in preferred stock of another U.S. corporation, the income received is dividends, not interest. These dividends may qualify for the Dividends-Received Deduction (DRD), which allows a corporation to exclude a portion of the dividends from taxable income. Current DRD rate at the time of writing this piece is:

- **50% deduction:** If the investing corporation owns less than 20% of the distributing corporation
- **65% deduction:** If ownership is 20% or more but less than 80%
- **100% deduction:** If ownership is 80% or more (treated as an affiliated group).

To qualify for the DRD, the preferred stock must generally be held for more than 45 days during a 91-day window surrounding the ex-dividend date. It should be pointed out that the DRD does not apply to:

- Debt-like preferred stock (e.g., "short-term" preferred with mandatory redemption).
- Dividends from REITs.
- Dividends from foreign corporations (unless specific treaties or rules apply).

For illustration suppose company A owns 10% of Corporation B's preferred stock. Corporation B pays $1,000,000 in preferred dividends. Corporate tax rate = 21% with a 50% DRD: Taxable income = $500,000, Tax owed = $105,000 Effective tax rate on dividends = 10.5% which is less than 21% corporate tax rate.

From a corporate finance and strategy viewpoint: Preferred stock can be tax-efficient relative to interest-bearing instruments. The DRD makes preferred dividends more attractive than bond interest, which is fully taxable. This is one reason preferred stock is commonly held by corporations and financial institutions, rather than individuals.

The management of corporate cash and assets is neither a passive nor a purely administrative function; rather, it is a critical element of corporate strategy. As another illustration, consider the strategic decision between owning a corporate asset—such as a building—and engaging in a sale-and-leaseback transaction for that same asset.

From a corporate strategy perspective, the decision to own real estate versus sell it and lease it back is not merely a financing choice; it is a decision that affects taxation, cash flows, balance sheet structure, and managerial flexibility.

When a corporation owns the building it uses for operation, the following may arise.

- **Depreciation:** The company can depreciate the building over its tax life (typically 39 years for commercial real estate in the U.S.).
- **Interest deduction:** If the building is financed with debt, interest payments are generally tax-deductible.
- **Operating expenses:** Maintenance, insurance, and property taxes are deductible.
- **Capital gains on sale:** Upon sale, the firm may incur capital gains tax and depreciation recapture at higher ordinary income rates.
- **From a strategic point of view:** Ownership provides control and stability; however, capital is tied up in a non-core asset, and tax benefits accrue gradually through depreciation.

In a sale-and-leaseback transaction, the firm sells the building to a third party and immediately leases it back for continued use.

- **Immediate taxable gain:** The sale may trigger capital gains tax (and depreciation recapture).
- **Lease payments fully deductible:** Rent payments are generally treated as operating expenses and are fully deductible for tax purposes.
- **No depreciation or interest deductions:** Since the firm no longer owns the asset, it cannot claim depreciation or interest deductions.

- **Off-balance-sheet effects (Historically):** While modern accounting standards (ASC 842/IFRS 16) require lease capitalisation, tax treatment still differs from ownership.

From a corporate strategy point of view, sales-leaseback converts illiquid real estate into immediate cash. It improves return on assets (ROA) and capital flexibility and shifts real estate risk to the lessor. Further, it often increases operating leverage due to fixed lease obligations.

The following table provides a summary of the cost-benefit analysis of ownership up real estate vs. sales-leaseback.

Benefits	Ownership	Sale-leaseback
Depreciation	Yes	No
Interest deduction	Yes (if debt-financed)	No
Rent deduction	No	Yes (100%)
Capital gains exposure	Deferred	Immediate
Balance sheet flexibility	Lower	Higher
Tax timing	Gradual	Accelerated

Lease payments often provide a faster tax shield than depreciation, especially for firms with high taxable income.

From a corporate strategy lens, the choice of ownership vs sale-leaseback depends on the cost of capital, tax position of the firm, opportunity cost of capital tied up in real estate, risk tolerance, and the need for liquidity. Many firms pursue sale-and-leasebacks when real estate is not a source of competitive advantage, management prefers to redeploy capital into core operations, and the after-tax cost of leasing is lower than owning.

To illustrate the tax and strategic implications of owning a corporate building versus engaging in a sale–leaseback transaction, consider the following simplified example.

Assume a corporation owns a commercial building with a market value of $300 million, which is also equal to its tax depreciation basis. The corporate tax rate is 21%, the firm's required rate of return (discount rate) is 6%, and the building is depreciated using straight-line depreciation over 39 years, consistent with U.S. tax rules for commercial real estate.

Tax shield from ownership
The annual depreciation expense is: 300,000,000/39
The annual tax shield from depreciation is therefore:

$$0.21 \times 300{,}000{,}000/39$$

The present value of the tax shield from depreciation over 39 years is:

$$\sum 0.21 \times (300{,}000{,}000/39)/(1+6\%)^i$$

At the end of the depreciation period, the building is assumed to have no remaining economic value apart from the land on which it sits. Land is not depreciable, but it may appreciate over time. The share of land value in a commercial property varies substantially by location and asset type: approximately 15–25% in suburban areas, 25–40% in urban locations, 40–60% or more in prime central business districts, 10–20% for industrial properties, and 30–50% for high-traffic retail sites.

For illustrative purposes, assume that land represents 25% of the property's initial value, or $75 million, and that land appreciates at an average annual inflation rate of f. The present value of the tax benefit associated with recovering this value at year 39 (through sale or continued ownership) is:

$$0.21 \times 75{,}000{,}000 \times (1+f)^{39}/(1+0.06)^{39}$$

Accordingly, the total tax shield from owning the building is the sum of the present value of depreciation tax shields and the discounted tax benefit associated with the land value at the end of the horizon.

Now consider an alternative strategy in which the company sells the building and leases it back under a 39-year lease with an annual lease payment of $20 million. Lease payments are fully tax deductible as operating expenses. The annual tax shield is therefore:

$$0.21 \times 20{,}000{,}0000$$

The present value of the tax shield under the lease arrangement is:

$$\sum 21 \times 20{,}000{,}000/(1+0.06)^i$$

Unlike ownership, the firm does not benefit from land appreciation under a sale–leaseback arrangement.

	Tax Shield			
Inflation rate (%)	**Owning**	**Capital freed**	**Sale-lease back**	**Capital freed**
2	\$39.92	\$0	\$62.79	\$300
3	\$46.55	\$0	\$62.79	\$300
4	\$55.87	\$0	\$62.79	\$300
5	\$68.91	\$0	\$62.79	\$300

A comparison of these tax shields under different inflation assumptions reveals an important strategic trade-off. In a low or subdued inflation environment, the present value of lease-related tax deductions typically exceeds the tax benefits associated with ownership, making sale–leaseback transactions financially attractive. By contrast, in a high-inflation environment, appreciation in land value can significantly enhance the after-tax economics of ownership, potentially making owning the building superior to leasing.

This analysis highlights a broader strategic insight: decisions such as sale–leaseback transactions should not be evaluated solely on current market conditions or accounting considerations. Instead, they must incorporate expectations about inflation, interest rates, and asset appreciation, and ideally assign probabilities to different macroeconomic regimes. In this sense, real estate decisions—like cash management and capital structure—are integral components of corporate strategy rather than purely tactical or administrative choices.

Sale–leaseback is neither inherently good nor bad. Its strategic value depends on timing, core business strength, and macroeconomic conditions. When aligned with a coherent corporate strategy, it enhances return on invested capital.

Linear programming is a quantitative optimization technique that is particularly useful in corporate strategy when firms seek to minimize total tax liability while operating across multiple jurisdictions with different tax regimes. It allows management to incorporate strategic, operational, and regulatory constraints into a single coherent decision framework. The following simplified example illustrates how linear programming can be applied to a multinational firm's manufacturing and tax-planning decisions.

Consider a company that produces 150 widgets per year. As part of its long-term corporate strategy, the firm intends to diversify its manufacturing footprint across two geographic locations in order to reduce operational risk, limit political or regulatory exposure, and avoid excessive concentration in any single jurisdiction. The two locations face different corporate tax rates: 21% in Location A and 18% in Location B.

Let:

$$A = \text{number of widgets manufactured in Location A}$$

$$B = \text{number of widgets manufactured in Location B}$$

To balance diversification and concentration risk, management imposes the following strategic constraints:

$A \geq 10$ (minimum production to ensure diversification)

$A \leq 60$ (upper limit to avoid excessive concentration)

$B \geq 25$ (minimum production to ensure diversification)

$B \leq 60$ (upper limit to avoid excessive concentration)

$A + B \leq 110$ (capacity constraint across the two locations)

$A + B \geq 80$ (minimum scale required for operational efficiency)

The firm's objective function is to determine the allocation of production across the two locations that minimizes total tax expense, subject to the above strategic and operational constraints. Since production in Location A is taxed at 21% and production in Location B at 18%, the objective function can be written as:

$$\text{Minimize} \quad 0.21A + 0.18B$$

Subject to the constraints listed above.

This problem can be illustrated graphically by plotting A on the horizontal (X) axis and B on the vertical (Y) axis. Each inequality defines a boundary in the A–B plane, and the intersection of all constraints forms a feasible region. The shaded (or darkened) area in the graph represents the set of all production combinations that satisfy the firm's strategic diversification requirements, capacity limitations, and scale constraints.

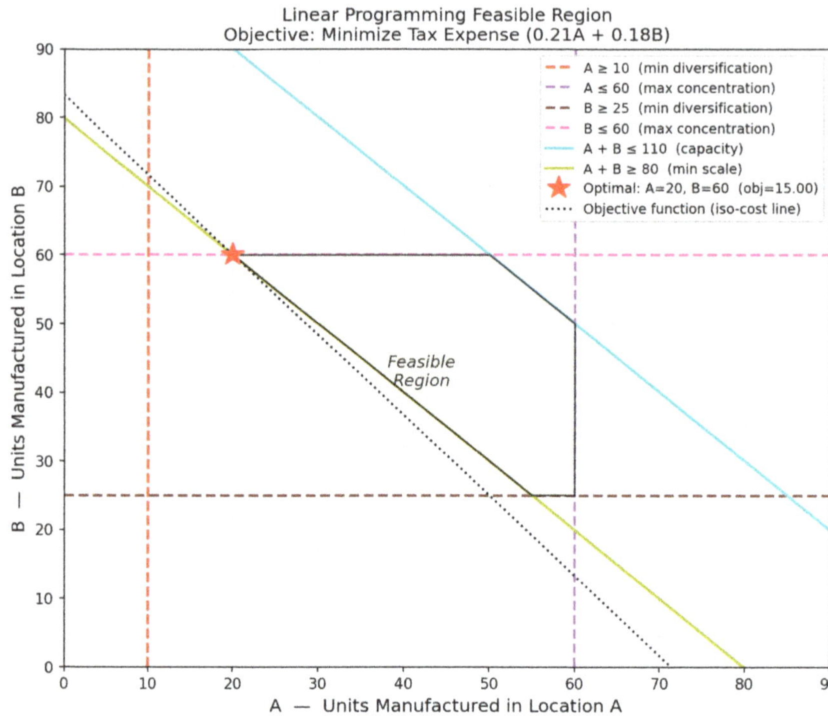

Within this feasible region, the optimal solution lies at one of the corner points, where the objective function reaches its minimum value. This reflects a fundamental property of linear programming: when both the objective function and constraints are linear, the optimal solution occurs at an extreme point of the feasible set.

From a corporate strategy perspective, this example highlights an important insight: tax minimization cannot be pursued in isolation. Instead, it must be balanced against diversification goals, capacity constraints, risk management considerations, and long-term strategic flexibility. Linear programming provides a disciplined and transparent framework for making such trade-offs explicit and analytically tractable.

The role of tax in corporate strategy encompasses various aspects. One aspect is to protect shareholders' profits by minimizing the amount paid to the government. Additionally, tax considerations are crucial in managing divestitures or spin-offs to avoid unfavorable tax consequences that may arise from such transactions. By carefully addressing these tax-related factors in a company's strategy, management can ensure that its actions create and do not destroy shareholder value.

The 2020 pandemic served as a stark reminder of the significance of a resilient supply chain. It revealed that even highly optimized supply chains can be vulnerable. This wake-up call prompted companies to prioritize diversification by sourcing supplies from various countries or continents. Consequently, the tax implications across different jurisdictions where a company operates became a critical consideration, emphasizing the need for tax-efficient diversification. Linear programming provides a solution to this challenge by facilitating the determination of an optimal diversification arrangement. Fortunately, a simple yet powerful tool, like Microsoft Excel, can be used to find the solution to a linear programming problem.

To illustrate this approach, we use a hypothetical example where a company decided to spread its operations among four countries. Let C_1, C_2, C_3, and C_4 be the percent of operations in each country, and θ_1, θ_2, θ_3, and θ_4 stand for the tax rates in each of these countries. Further, to achieve diversification at least 5% of production should be in each country and no two countries should produce more than 70% of total production. Following is the casting of the above question in a linear programming framework that can be solved using EXCEL.

$$\text{Minimize } Z = \theta_1 C_1 + \theta_2 C_2 + \theta_3 C_3 + \theta_4 C_4$$

$$\begin{aligned}
\text{s.t. } & C_1 + C_2 + C_3 + C_4 = 100\% \\
& C_1 + C_2 \leq 70\% \\
& C_1 + C_3 \leq 70\% \\
& C_1 + C_4 \leq 70\% \\
& C_2 + C_3 \leq 70\% \\
& C_2 + C_4 \leq 70\% \\
& C_3 + C_4 \leq 70\% \\
& C_1 \geq 5\%, C_2 \geq 5\%, C_3 \geq 5\%, C_4 \geq 5\%
\end{aligned}$$

A step-by-step tutorial on solving this model in Excel is offered at the end of this chapter.

The realm of taxation extends beyond corporate tax alone; it encompasses various aspects, such as the tax treatment of lease agreements and actions associated with spinning off specific operations. These considerations, however, delve into case-specific scenarios, yet they hold significant importance in the design of corporate strategies. Evaluating the potential tax implications of these factors is crucial to ensure a well-informed and effective approach, considering the potential consequences for both the company and its shareholders. By incorporating these considerations into strategic decision-making, companies can navigate tax-related complexities and optimize their overall corporate strategy.

Using Microsoft Excel to Solve Linear Programming

1. Set Up the Problem in Excel

Decision Variables: Define cells for C_1, C_2, C_3, and $C4$, which will represent the percentage allocation for each variable.

Objective Function: Have another cell that computes the function $Z = \theta_1 C_1 + \theta_2 C_2 + \theta_3 C_3 + \theta_4 C_4$

Constraints: Set up cells that represent each constraint. For example:

- A cell representing $C_1 + C_2 + C_3 + C_4$ which should equal 100%.
- Another cell representing $C_1 + C_2$, which should be $\leq 70\%$.

... and so on.

2. Install and Activate Solver

If not already done, activate the Solver tool following the previous steps.

3. Using Solver

- Click on "Solver" in the "Data" tab.
- Set your objective by selecting the cell that represents your function Z.
- Choose Min since you're minimizing the objective function.
- By changing variable cells, select the range of cells representing your decision variables ($C1$, $C2$, $C3$, $C4$).
- Add constraints by clicking on the "Add" button and setting up each constraint as mentioned in the problem. Remember to also set the constraints for each variable being $\geq 5\%$.
- Once all constraints are added, click OK.

- In the Solver Parameters dialog box, choose a solving method. For LP problems, Simplex LP is recommended.
- Click Solve.

4. Review and Implement Results

- Solver will provide the optimal allocation for $C1$, $C2$, $C3$, and $C4$ that minimizes Z while adhering to the constraints.
- Review the solution and decide whether to keep the solver solution or revert to original values.

5. Save and Finish

Save your workbook.

You've now set up and solved your specific linear programming problem in Excel!

Chapter 6

Debt

Debts are like children - begot with pleasure, but brought forth with pain.

— Moliere

In 1948, seeking to cash in on the post-World War II baby boom, Charles Lazarus opened his first store in Washington, D.C. called "Children's Bargain Town," specializing in cribs and strollers. Recognizing the potential in the toy market, Lazarus expanded his inventory to include toys alongside baby products. In 1957, he rebranded the store as "Toys "R" Us." Setting itself apart from department stores with limited toy selections, Toys "R" Us gained traction by offering a diverse range of toys at affordable prices.

During the 1960s and 1970s, Toys "R" Us experienced remarkable growth, establishing a strong presence across the United States. The company revolutionized the retail landscape with its large-scale toy stores, providing extensive product choices and a delightful shopping experience for families. Embarking on the strategy of expanding internationally in the 1980s, Toys "R" Us opened stores in Canada, the United Kingdom, and other countries, captivating customers worldwide with its wide array of toys and dedicated toy shopping atmosphere.

In 2009, Toys "R" Us solidified its position as a leading toy retailer by acquiring the rights to the esteemed FAO Schwarz brand, renowned for its iconic flagship store in New York City. This strategic acquisition further bolstered the company's market presence.

Toys "R" Us' expansion was mainly fueled by debt which has several advantages over means of financing, including tax advantages and not diluting shareholders' ownership. However, extensive borrowing can overburden firm and jeopardize its financial health, as it did in the case of Toys "R" Us. Coupled with fierce competition from online retailers, Toys "R" Us encountered significant challenges. These factors ultimately forced the company into bankruptcy in 2017, as it struggled to service its debt amidst the rapidly evolving retail landscape.

Price of Toys R Us bonds maturing October 2018.

Excessive debt and leveraged capital structure can derail even the most promising strategy, as demonstrated by the case of AT&T. Under the leadership of CEO Randall Stephenson, AT&T pursued a strategy to enter the content business as a means of revenue growth. This involved acquiring prominent content providers such as Time Warner, HBO, and DirecTV, with the total cost of these acquisitions reaching billions of dollars. However, the funding for these transactions heavily relied on debt issuance, resulting in a substantial accumulation of debt for AT&T.

At its peak, AT&T's outstanding debt exceeded $180 billion, leading to a highly leveraged capital structure. This significant debt burden strained the company's financial resources and increased its interest expenses. While such a capital structure might have seemed justifiable in a low-interest-rate environment, it became unsustainable as interest rates started to rise. It became evident that the strategy and its funding approach were no longer viable.

Under the leadership of the new CEO John Stankey, AT&T made a strategic shift. Recognizing the need to address the debt burden, the company opted to sell certain assets and utilize the proceeds to reduce its debt load. The decision to sell businesses, including Warner Media assets and enter a partnership with Discovery, was primarily driven by the objective of alleviating the debt burden. This allowed AT&T to refocus on its core competencies in the telecommunications industry, specifically wireless, broadband, and 5G networks. The divestment of content-related businesses aimed to streamline operations and concentrate on areas where AT&T possessed strengths.

In summary, the combination of excessive debt and an inappropriate capital structure undermined AT&T's initial strategy of entering the content business. Despite the potential merits of the strategy, the clash between the telecommunications and entertainment cultures further complicated its implementation. The subsequent restructuring efforts, including asset sales and debt reduction, aimed to rectify the situation and enable AT&T to refocus on its core competencies.

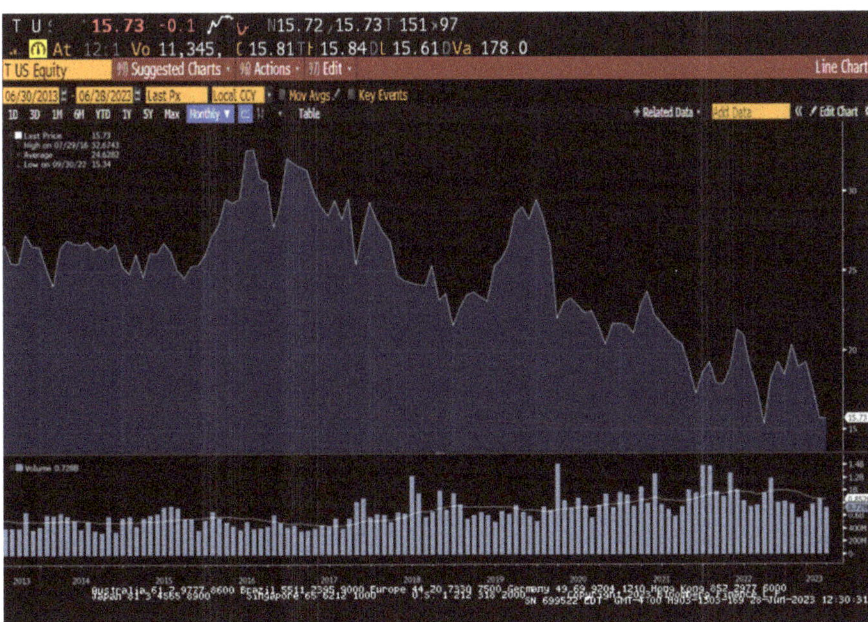

As these examples show, while debt can fuel growth of firms and support their various strategic moves, the extent of reliance on debt (i.e., leverage) needs to be carefully analyzed.

In order to systematically examine this topic and offer guidelines that can aid in strategy, let us begin with the fundamental principles. Let us envision a firm as a system, illustrated in the following figure.

Human capital refers to the individuals employed by a company, while financial capital is necessary for acquiring production resources such as inventory, plants, and machinery. This capital is provided by investors through the capital market. However, it is important to note that the investor community is not homogeneous. Retirees, for instance, tend to be risk-averse and prioritize the preservation of their principal, while venture capitalists seek high returns relative to the risks associated with startup investments. A vibrant capital market serves the crucial function of catering to different segments of investors by creating financial products and instruments with diverse risk-reward profiles.

Debt and equity are the two primary types of funding available. Additionally, there are hybrid instruments that possess characteristics of both debt and equity. Convertible bonds, for example, exhibit equity features, while preferred shares bear fixed income characteristics.

Debt and equity differ significantly in terms of risk and reward. When a company issues a bond, for instance, the payment of interest and principal becomes a legal obligation, and failure to meet these obligations can result in the company being forced into bankruptcy by bondholders. In contrast, dividend payments to shareholders are discretionary and not obligatory. Therefore, a heavy debt burden increases the likelihood of a firm struggling to meet interest or principal payments, leading to financial distress. Consequently, lenders and rating agencies closely monitor a company's financial leverage, represented by the debt-to-equity ratio, as they evaluate and monitor its creditworthiness.

The combination of debt and equity constitutes the capital structure of a company. It is essential for companies to strike a balance between debt and equity components to maintain a sustainable and robust financial position.

In the US, the Securities and Exchange Commission (SEC) mandates that public companies must release their 10-Q report on a quarterly basis, which serves as their income statement, and their 10-K report annually, which presents their balance sheet. These reports contain essential information that investors and market participants utilize, along with other data, to assess the company's performance, overall value, and creditworthiness. Within the income statement, particular figures of interest include the Profit or Net Income (= profit) and earnings per share (P/e).

The board of directors holds the authority to determine the allocation of profits between dividends for shareholders, known as the payout ratio, and reinvestment into the company for potential growth projects. They have the discretion to choose whether to return a portion of the profit to equity holders through dividends or share buybacks. The remaining funds can be utilized to fuel the company's growth initiatives. This retained portion of profit belongs to shareholders, and its utilization for projects is evaluated through the Return on Invested Capital (ROIC), which measures the effectiveness of the management's growth strategy. Investors anticipate a return on their investment as compensation for the risk they undertake, knowing that the company may face failure and they could potentially lose some or all of their invested capital.

Paying careful attention to the nature of the business and its position within a company's life cycle is crucial when formulating a business strategy and the resulting capital structure. To illustrate this point, let's consider the example of an IT start-up funded by Venture Capital (VC) that currently lacks a product and hence revenue and is burning cash, with the VC contemplating an exit strategy through an Initial Public Offering (IPO). In such a scenario, it is neither advisable nor cost-effective and probably not possible for the company to raise capital through a bank loan or issuance of bonds. The interest rates for such borrowing would be prohibitively high, as lenders would be assuming substantial risk regarding the company's ability to generate sufficient cash flows in the future to meet interest and principal payments.

Now, let's compare this start-up with an oil company operating in a mature industry, benefiting from healthy revenue generated by selling various refined products produced by its refineries. These products are consistently in demand. Given the company's stable cash flows and valuable hard assets, such as land and machinery, raising capital through borrowing at favorable rates is feasible because the lenders note that in the event of bankruptcy, the company's assets hold significant value, and the recovery rates would be high.

Clearly, the business strategies and resulting capital structures of these two companies will differ significantly. Consequently, determining the optimal capital structure should be based on the company's position within the business life cycle, as depicted in following figure.

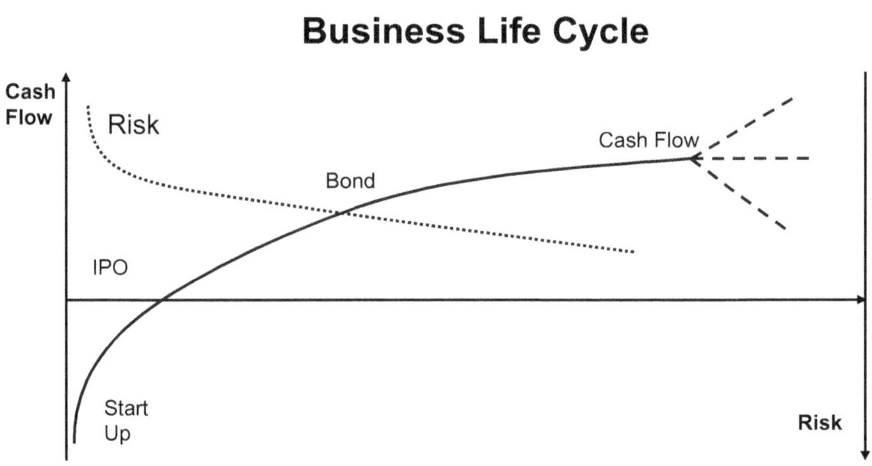

There are four major reasons that corporate strategy could result in adjusting the company's capital structure.

1. Enhancing ROE (Return on Equity) through strategic leverage. It's worth noting that ROE can be improved by utilizing financial leverage.

$$\begin{aligned} \text{Note that ROE} &= (\text{Earnings/Equity}) = (\text{Earnings/Assets})\ (\text{Assets/Equity}) \\ &= (\text{Return/Assets})\ (\text{Equity} + \text{Debt})/\text{Equity} \\ &= \text{ROA}\ (1 + \text{Financial Leverage}). \end{aligned}$$

The additional funds obtained through leveraging can be allocated towards various purposes, such as share buybacks, increased dividends, or one-time extraordinary dividends. However, management should exercise caution and consider the implications of additional interest expenses, as well cost of future debt refinancing, particularly in the event of higher general interest rates or a widened the credit spread of the company or both.

2. **Acquisition**: Companies resort to debt financing to raise capital for the purpose of acquiring other companies, thereby driving revenue growth, diversifying their business, entering new markets, and achieving vertical integration, among other strategic objectives. However, this approach comes with inherent risks. There is a possibility that the projected increase in revenue may not materialize as expected, integration of the acquired company may encounter challenges, and the burden of interest payments on the additional borrowings may become onerous. Furthermore, during an economic downturn or in the face of stiff competition, the company may struggle to service the debt, potentially leading to financial distress.

3. **Expansion**: Capital is often raised with the intention of enhancing, streamlining, and reorganizing operations, venturing into new business lines, and upgrading and modernizing manufacturing processes. In such instances, it is crucial for management to study and scrutinize the assumptions underlying the forecasts regarding the potential impact of these endeavors. Additionally, it is essential to assess the company's ability to effectively service the debt incurred as a result of these initiatives. Careful evaluation of these factors is imperative to ensure that the anticipated benefits are realized and that the company remains financially stable in the long run.

4. **Divestiture**: The company strategically divests assets or spins off businesses with the objective of reducing its debt and alleviating the interest burden. By selling off assets or creating separate entities, the company aims to generate funds that can be utilized to make debt payments and improve its overall financial position. This approach enables the company to streamline its operations and focus on core areas of strength, while simultaneously reducing the financial strain associated with servicing excessive debt.

Chapter 7

Depreciation & Amortization

> Accelerated depreciation helps companies bring forward capital-intensive investments by reducing payback time. It's not a hand out. Companies still have to pay the tax, but they simply get to defer it.
>
> — Anothony Pratt

The COVID-19 pandemic had a profound impact on various aspects of people's lives, and one of the severely affected industries was the travel sector. Marriott International, one of the largest hotel chains globally, experienced a significant decline in revenue in 2020 as a result. Relative to the previous year, the company's revenue dropped by almost 50%, which had a substantial effect on its financial performance. Consequently, Marriott International's stock also witnessed a steep decline of approximately 50% during that period.

To navigate the challenging circumstances caused by the pandemic, Marriott International strategically employed various financial tools, including depreciation. Depreciation is a non-cash item that allows companies to allocate the cost of their tangible assets over their estimated useful lives. By leveraging this accounting practice effectively, Marriott International was able to reduce its earnings before interest and tax (EBIT) to $434 million, representing a substantial portion of its EBITDA (Earnings Before Interest, Tax, Depreciation, and Amortization), which stood at $1,069 million.

By utilizing depreciation in this manner, Marriott International could present a lower EBIT figure, reflecting the impact of the pandemic on its operations. This strategic use of depreciation helped mitigate the company's financial challenges during the unprecedented downturn in the travel industry caused by the pandemic.

It's worth noting that while depreciation is a valuable accounting tool to spread the costs of assets over time, it does not directly impact a company's cash flow. The reduction in EBIT resulting from the depreciation expense was a non-cash item, meaning it did not involve an actual outflow of funds.

Almost half of the world's oil is consumed for transportation purposes. The COVID-19 pandemic had a profound impact on the travel industry, leading to a significant decrease in global road travel and commercial flight activity. During the first year of the pandemic, road travel declined by approximately 50%, while commercial flights experienced a staggering 60% reduction compared to pre-pandemic levels. This decline in travel had severe consequences for the airline industry, with many carriers facing the risk of bankruptcy. One example is American Airlines, whose stock price in 2020 dropped by over 80% compared to its value in 2018.

The airline industry's struggles were further exemplified by unprecedented events in the oil market. Due to plummeting demand and storage capacity constraints, oil futures, for the first time in history, were sold at negative prices. This meant that those holding long oil contracts had to pay someone to take the oil off their hands.

ExxonMobil, the largest oil company in the United States, also faced significant challenges during this period. The company experienced a 30% decline in revenue in 2020 compared to the previous year and witnessed a 70% drop in its share price.

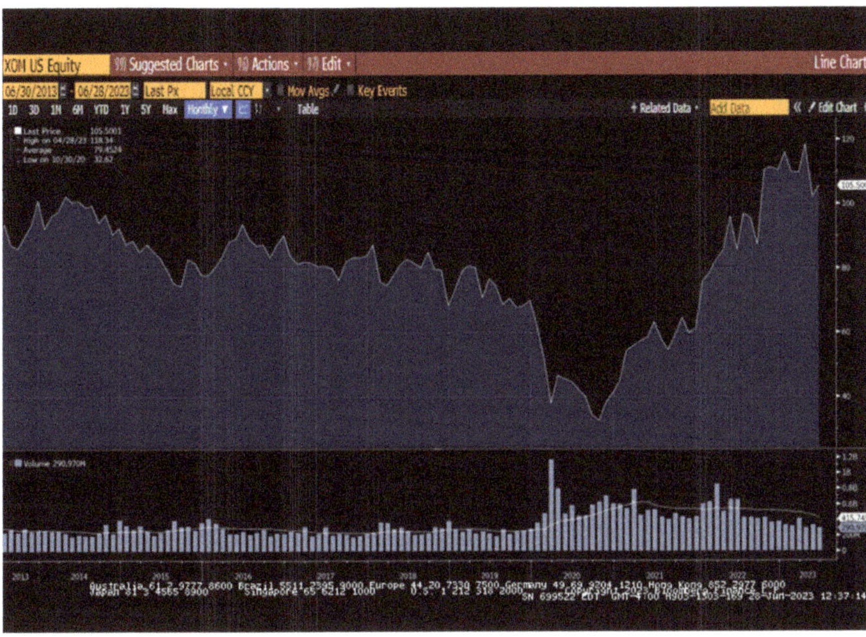

To mitigate the financial impact and alleviate the strain on its revenue, ExxonMobil implemented a depreciation strategy. The company depreciated over $46 billion worth of its assets, nearly 2.5 times the amount depreciated the year before. This strategic use of depreciation resulted in an Earnings Before Interest and Taxes (EBIT) of −$4.8 billion for ExxonMobil, effectively reducing its taxable income and resulting in no tax liability for that year.

By employing depreciation as a financial tool, ExxonMobil was able to offset the negative effects of the pandemic on its revenue and navigate the challenging market conditions in the oil industry.

Companies can utilize amortization and depreciation strategies to effectively lower their taxable income and reduce tax liabilities. Here are a few examples of companies that have implemented such strategies:

- **Technology Companies:** Technology companies often invest heavily in research and development (R&D) to innovate and develop new products. They can take advantage of amortization rules to spread the costs of R&D over time, reducing their taxable income. For instance, software companies may amortize the costs associated with developing software products.
- **Real Estate Companies:** Real estate companies frequently benefit from depreciation deductions on their properties. They can depreciate the cost of buildings, improvements, and other tangible assets over time, reducing their taxable income. This allows them to offset rental income and lower their tax obligations.
- **Airlines:** Airlines invest substantial amounts in purchasing aircraft, which can be depreciated over a specified period. Depreciation on these assets helps reduce their taxable income, offsetting their operating costs and enhancing their financial performance.
- **Manufacturing Companies:** Manufacturers often rely on heavy machinery, equipment, and production facilities. They can depreciate these assets over time, deducting a portion of their costs each year. This lowers their taxable income and assists in managing tax liabilities effectively.
- **Energy Companies:** Companies operating in the energy sector, such as oil and gas exploration and production, often have significant capital investments in infrastructure and equipment. They can employ depreciation strategies to offset their expenses and lower their tax burden.

It's important to note that tax strategies can be complex and subject to specific regulations and guidelines in different jurisdictions. The examples provided highlight how certain industries and companies can leverage amortization and depreciation effectively to reduce taxes, but the specific implementation and impact may vary based on individual circumstances and applicable tax laws.

Chapter 8

Operating Expenses

Control your expenses better than your competition.
This is where you can always find the competitive advantage.

— Sam Walton

At the turn of the 21st century, General Electric (GE) stood as the last of the original Dow Jones companies that had also existed at the start of the 20th century. Founded in 1892 through the merger of the Edison General Electric Company and the Thomson-Houston Electric Company, GE's early years were characterized by remarkable innovations in electrical power and lighting, including the incandescent light bulb. Throughout the early 1900s, GE expanded its operations across various sectors, such as transportation, aviation, and industrial products. The company played a pivotal role in electrifying America and contributed to advancements in electrical infrastructure. Notably, GE made significant contributions during World War II by producing military equipment and technology.

Continuing its growth trajectory, GE diversified and expanded globally, venturing into industries such as appliances, medical equipment, power generation, and finance. Under the leadership of legendary CEO Jack Welch, GE transformed into a multinational conglomerate, achieving remarkable success in the finance and banking sectors. Welch's tenure saw GE's market value soar from less than $15 billion in 1981 to a peak of $594 billion in 2000. At its peak, GE Capital, the financial services division of GE, contributed to more than 40% of the company's revenue.

However, the great credit recession and subprime financial crisis of 2008 dealt a severe blow to GE. The company's stock price plummeted by 40%, leading to dividend cuts and significant challenges. In response, the GE Board of Directors appointed Larry Culp as the CEO and Chairman on October 1, 2018, making him the first outsider to lead the company in its history.

Under Culp's leadership, a comprehensive turnaround strategy was implemented. Efforts were made to reduce the company's debt and enhance liquidity through divestitures of non-core businesses, such as the sale of the biopharma business to Danaher. Cost-cutting measures were adopted to improve profitability, and a renewed focus was placed on GE's core industrial strengths, including power, aviation, and renewable energy, where the company had a competitive advantage and growth potential. Streamlining processes, boosting productivity, and driving down costs became key priorities, resulting in initiatives like lean manufacturing practices, supply chain optimization, and digital transformation to enhance operational performance.

The following charts highlight the contrasting performance of IBM, an esteemed and long-established company in the computing and information technology industry, when compared to relatively newer players like Apple and Microsoft. Over the past decade, while the stock prices of Microsoft and Apple have surged, experiencing a tenfold increase, IBM's stock price has encountered a decline of 30%.

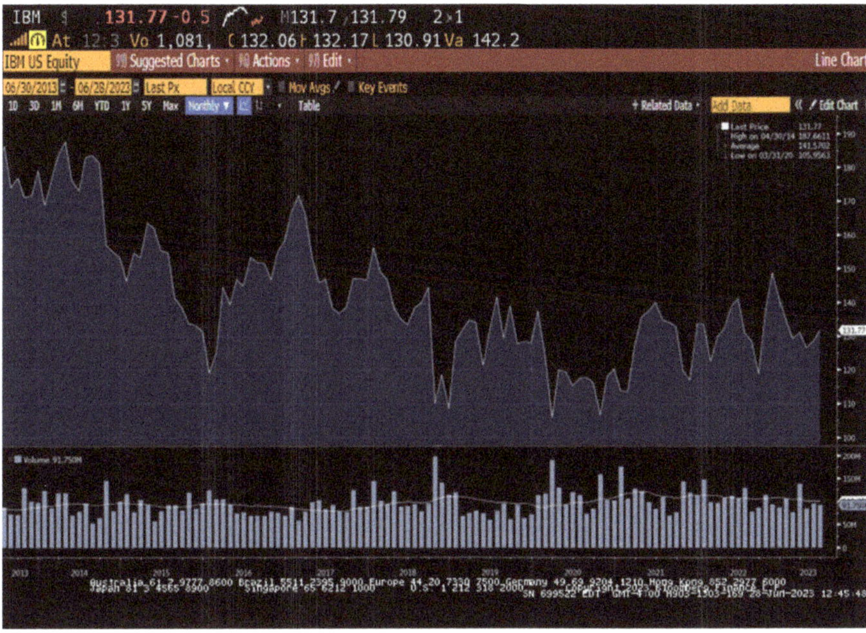

This decline can be attributed, at least in part, to IBM's strategic missteps in failing to fully recognize the significance of cloud computing and placing excessive emphasis on leveraging Watson as a growth driver.

IBM, as a pioneer in the industry, has a rich history and legacy. However, the company faced challenges in adapting to the evolving technological landscape. The rapid growth of cloud computing, which has transformed the IT industry, presented a lucrative opportunity for companies like Microsoft and Amazon. Unfortunately, IBM's focus on using Watson, its cognitive computing system, as a primary growth engine proved to be a bad strategy.

Cloud computing emerged as a game-changer, providing scalable and cost-effective solutions for businesses and individuals. Microsoft and Amazon successfully recognized this shift and strategically positioned themselves in the cloud computing market, enabling them to capture substantial growth and investor confidence. In contrast, IBM's delayed response to the growing importance of cloud computing hindered its ability to compete effectively in this rapidly expanding sector.

IBM has undertaken a series of strategic adjustments to position itself for success in the evolving market landscape. One of the key areas of focus for IBM has been cloud computing and cognitive solutions, including artificial intelligence and data analytics. By embracing these high-growth areas, IBM has been able to leverage its expertise in advanced technologies, potentially leading to cost savings and improved profitability.

To enhance its operations and reduce operating expenses, IBM has implemented various initiatives—cost management has been a priority for IBM. The company has taken a proactive approach to monitor expenses throughout its operations. One notable effort has been workforce restructuring, aimed at optimizing the organizational structure and aligning the workforce with current business needs. This has involved measures such as workforce reductions, early retirement programs, and reshaping the employee base to concentrate on key growth areas.

Additionally, IBM has embarked on streamlining its operations and concentrating on its core strengths. As part of this strategy, the company has pursued divestitures of non-core businesses, reducing costs associated with maintaining diverse business segments. This allows IBM to focus its resources on areas that align more closely with its strategic objectives.

Furthermore, IBM has recognized the importance of operational efficiency and has actively pursued initiatives to improve workflows and eliminate waste. The company is implementing lean methodologies, automation, and digital transformation initiatives to streamline processes, enhance productivity, and achieve overall operational efficiency.

To further elaborate on these points, note that since cash is the lifeblood of any business, companies are obligated to present a statement of cash flows alongside their financial statements to accurately depict their cash position. The statement of cash flows provides a comprehensive overview of the inflows and outflows of cash within the organization and helps stakeholders understand how cash is generated and utilized.

The statement of cash flow encompasses three main categories: operating activities, investing activities, and financing activities. Each category accounts for specific cash inflows and outflows that contribute to the overall cash position of the company.

- **Operating Activities:** This category encompasses cash flows generated from the core operations of the business. It includes cash receipts from sales, interest, and dividends received, as well as cash payments for expenses such as salaries, inventory, and taxes. Operating activities demonstrate the company's ability to generate cash from its primary operations.
- **Investing Activities:** This category focuses on cash flows related to investments in long-term assets and other ventures. It includes cash receipts from the sale of assets, interest, and dividends received from investments, as well as cash payments for the acquisition of new assets, investments, and loans made to others. Investing activities highlight the company's investment decisions and their impact on cash flow.
- **Financing Activities:** This category covers cash flows associated with obtaining and repaying capital. It includes cash inflows from issuing stocks or bonds, borrowing funds, and receiving contributions from owners, as well as cash outflows from dividends paid, debt repayments, and stock repurchases. Financing activities reflect the company's financing structure and how it raises and returns capital.

Many factors such as interest rates, tax rates, customer demand, and the cost of funds is beyond the control of management on the other hand elements such as operating expenses fall under the jurisdiction of management.

The external factors mentioned above, such as interest rates and tax rates, are determined by economic conditions and government regulations, which are beyond the direct control of management. Likewise, customer demand is influenced by various market dynamics, consumer preferences, and competitive forces. The cost of funds, including borrowing rates and access to capital, is impacted by financial markets and the overall economic climate. These external elements collectively shape the business environment in which the company operates.

However, the elements within the box represent the operational aspects of the business that can be directly controlled and managed by the organization's management team. Operations encompass activities such as production, supply chain management, human resources, marketing, and other internal processes. Management has the authority and responsibility to make strategic decisions, allocate resources, and optimize these operational functions to achieve organizational goals and objectives.

The strategy for operations of a business usually deals with some of the following categories:

- **Process Optimization:** Analyzing and improving existing processes is crucial for enhancing operational efficiency. This involves identifying bottlenecks, streamlining workflows, eliminating redundant steps, and automating manual tasks. Process optimization can lead to cost savings, reduced cycle times, improved quality, and increased customer satisfaction.
- **Technology Adoption:** Leveraging technology solutions can significantly improve operations. Implementing enterprise resource planning (ERP) systems, customer relationship management (CRM) software, supply chain management tools, and data analytics platforms can enhance productivity, enable better decision-making, and facilitate seamless collaboration across departments.
- **Lean Methodologies:** Applying lean principles, such as just-in-time production, waste reduction, and continuous improvement, can help eliminate inefficiencies and maximize value. Lean methodologies focus on reducing non-value-added activities, optimizing resource utilization, and creating a culture of continuous process enhancement.
- **Quality Management:** Emphasizing quality throughout the organization can yield significant operational improvements. Implementing quality control measures, conducting regular inspections, and fostering a culture of quality can minimize defects, improve customer satisfaction, and reduce rework or returns.
- **Supply Chain Optimization:** Enhancing the efficiency and effectiveness of the supply chain can have a substantial impact on overall operations. This involves optimizing inventory levels, improving supplier relationships, implementing demand forecasting, and adopting efficient logistics and distribution practices.
- **Employee Training and Development:** Investing in the development of employees is crucial for operational excellence. Providing training programs, fostering a culture of learning, and encouraging skill development can enhance employee performance, increase productivity, and promote innovation within the organization.
- **Performance Measurement and KPIs:** Establishing key performance indicators (KPIs) and implementing regular performance measurement systems allow organizations to monitor progress, identify areas for

improvement, and align operations with strategic goals. This data-driven approach enables better decision-making and facilitates targeted operational enhancements.

- **Continuous Improvement Culture:** Creating a culture of continuous improvement encourages employees at all levels to identify and propose operational enhancements. Implementing regular feedback mechanisms, conducting employee engagement initiatives, and recognizing and rewarding innovative ideas can foster a culture of continuous learning and improvement.
- **Right-Sizing a Business by Changing Its Focus or Number of Employees or Hiring Workers with Different Skills:** Right-sizing refers to making adjustments to the size or structure of a business in order to align it more effectively with its goals and objectives. This can be achieved through various means. One approach is changing the business's focus, which involves shifting its strategic direction or reallocating resources to areas that offer better growth potential or higher profitability. For example, a company may decide to expand into a new market segment or invest more heavily in research and development.
  - Another aspect of right-sizing is adjusting the number of employees. This can involve both downsizing and upsizing. Downsizing may occur when a business needs to reduce its workforce due to factors such as cost-cutting measures, technological advancements that automate certain tasks, or changes in market demand. Upsizing, on the other hand, may involve hiring more employees to support business expansion or to fill skill gaps.
  - Hiring workers with different skills is another component of right-sizing. As businesses evolve, they may require employees with new or different skill sets to meet changing demands. This could involve recruiting individuals with expertise in emerging technologies, data analysis, or other specialized areas that align with the company's strategic objectives. By adapting the workforce's skill composition, businesses can enhance their ability to thrive in a rapidly evolving market landscape.
- **Selling Off, Spinning Off, or Discontinuing Certain Non-Core Businesses:** Businesses often undergo strategic evaluations to identify areas that are not considered core to their operations or do not align with their long-term objectives. In such cases, companies may choose to divest

or discontinue these non-core businesses. There are several options for achieving this:

- **Selling off:** This involves finding a buyer or investor who is interested in acquiring the non-core business or its assets. Selling off can be a strategic move to generate capital, streamline operations, or focus resources on core areas of expertise. The proceeds from the sale can be reinvested in the core business or used to reduce debt.
- **Spinning off:** A spinoff refers to creating a separate, independent entity out of a non-core business division. This allows the spun-off entity to operate autonomously and pursue its own strategic direction. The parent company typically distributes shares of the new entity to its existing shareholders, who then become shareholders of both the parent company and the spinoff. This strategy allows each entity to focus on its respective strengths and priorities.
- **Discontinuing:** In some cases, a non-core business may be discontinued entirely. This means ceasing its operations and winding down its activities. Discontinuation may occur when the business is no longer viable, is consistently unprofitable, or no longer fits within the company's strategic vision. This decision allows the company to redirect its resources and efforts toward more promising areas.
- **Headcount reduction for certain activities due to discontinuation or spinoff:** When a non-core business is discontinued or spun off, it often results in a reduced need for employees who were specifically engaged in supporting that business activity. In such situations, headcount reduction may be necessary. This involves downsizing the workforce by eliminating positions or transferring employees to other roles within the organization.

Headcount reduction can be a challenging process, as it impacts employees directly. Companies typically follow proper procedures, such as providing adequate notice, offering severance packages, and providing support in finding new employment opportunities. The goal is to minimize the negative impact on employees while aligning the workforce with the organization's revised strategic direction.

It's important to note that these strategic actions, such as right-sizing, divestment, and headcount reduction, should be carried out with careful planning and consideration of the potential impacts on employees, stakeholders, and the overall business.

It's important to note that the specific strategies for improving operations will vary depending on the nature of the business, industry, and organizational goals. Assessing the current state of operations, conducting thorough analysis, and involving key stakeholders in the improvement process are essential steps for implementing successful operational enhancements.

Chapter 9

Gross Profit Margin

Look for companies with high profit margin.

— Warren Buffett

It is widely recognized that Nestlé, a multinational food and beverage company, has an extensive product portfolio that appeals to a vast consumer base. In fact, it is estimated that a significant portion of the population in OECD countries consumes at least one of Nestlé's products. With over 2,000 brands under its umbrella, Nestlé offers a diverse range of products spanning various categories.

Nestlé's product lineup encompasses a wide array of consumer favorites, from globally recognized coffee brands like Nescafé to indulgent chocolate treats like KitKat and Smarties. The company's reach extends beyond traditional food items, as it also caters to other segments such as frozen foods with brands like Stouffer's and DiGiorno. Additionally, Nestlé takes care of the nutritional needs of infants with its NAN range of infant formulas and offers pet food products under the trusted Purina brand for the well-being of cats and dogs.

Notably, Nestlé's profitability and stability are highly regarded within the industry. The company consistently achieves a gross margin of 40%, which reflects its ability to generate substantial profits relative to its production costs. This robust margin is indicative of Nestlé's strong market position, effective pricing strategies, and operational efficiency.

Furthermore, Nestlé's financial performance demonstrates a consistent growth trajectory and long-standing profitability. The company has sustained its success over time, continuously generating positive financial results. This enduring profitability can perhaps signify Nestlé's strategic management, innovation capabilities, and its ability to adapt to evolving consumer preferences and market dynamics. Maintaining such a high gross margin in the food and beverage industry is no small feat, and Nestlé's achievement speaks to its ability to deliver products that consumers value and are willing to pay a premium for. This success also underscores Nestlé's dedication to quality, innovation, and meeting the diverse needs of its global customer base.

If you attend sporting events such as tennis or basketball, you cannot miss the ubiquitous presence of the Nike logo adorning the shirts, shorts, or sneakers of the players. Nike has solidified its position as one of the most prominent names in sportswear, and its products are sought after by athletes and consumers worldwide. The brand recognition that Nike has achieved provides the company with a significant advantage, leading to gross profit margins that consistently exceed 40%.

Nike's strong association with sports and its endorsement of top athletes have elevated its brand to iconic status. The famous Nike "swoosh" logo has become synonymous with performance, quality, and style in the sports industry. Seeing athletes at the pinnacle of their game donning Nike gear creates a powerful association between the brand and excellence, further reinforcing its reputation.

This brand recognition and association with sporting success have propelled Nike's products to global demand. From its innovative footwear, including iconic lines such as Air Jordan and Nike Air Max, to its stylish and functional apparel, Nike consistently delivers products that resonate with athletes, fitness enthusiasts, and fashion-conscious individuals alike. The company's ability to capture the spirit of athleticism while embracing evolving trends has solidified its appeal across diverse consumer segments.

Nike's strong brand equity has translated into a significant competitive advantage in the market. The desirability of the Nike brand has enabled the company to maintain premium pricing, ensuring healthy profit margins. With consumers willing to pay a premium for the Nike logo, the company enjoys strong revenue streams and the ability to invest in research, development, and marketing to further enhance its offerings.

Furthermore, Nike's success is not limited to its core product offerings. The brand's influence extends beyond sportswear, with collaborations, endorsements, and marketing campaigns that capture global attention. By associating itself with cultural icons, events, and social causes, Nike continually reinforces its brand image, expanding its reach and reinforcing its position as a leader in the industry.

In summary, Nike's pervasive presence in the world of sports, its globally recognized brand, and its ability to deliver products that resonate with consumers have contributed to its exceptional gross profit margins exceeding 40%. By leveraging its brand equity, staying attuned to market trends, and consistently delivering innovative and high-quality products, Nike has established itself as an iconic and profitable player in the sportswear industry.

The above cases suggest a positive correlation between high gross margins and the profitability of companies. Gross margin is a financial metric that represents the percentage of revenue left after deducting the direct costs associated with producing or delivering a product or service. It serves as an indicator of a company's ability to generate profit from its core operations.

When a company has a high gross margin, it means that it is able to sell its products or services at a significant markup over the direct costs of production. This provides the company with a larger buffer to cover other operating expenses, such as marketing, research and development, administration, and overhead costs. Consequently, a high gross margin can contribute to higher profitability. A high gross margin allows a company to allocate a larger portion of its revenue towards covering operating expenses. This provides more flexibility to invest in growth initiatives, innovation, marketing campaigns, or other activities that can drive sales and enhance the overall profitability of the company.

A high gross margin can also indicate that a company has a competitive advantage over its peers. This advantage could stem from factors like economies of scale, proprietary technology, or strong customer loyalty. Such advantages can translate into sustainable profitability, as the company can maintain healthy margins while remaining resilient to price competition.

Finally, companies with high gross margins have more financial resources available to reinvest in the business. These funds can be allocated towards research and development, expanding production capacity, acquiring new technologies, or entering new markets. These strategic investments can drive long-term growth and enhance profitability. Therefore, increasing gross margin should be an important idea in the strategic plan of a company. However, it is important to note that gross margin alone does not guarantee overall profitability. A company must also effectively manage its operating expenses, taxes, financing costs, and other factors that impact the bottom line. Additionally, the correlation between gross margin and profitability can vary across industries and market conditions.

Chapter 10

Asset Turnover

Asset turnover is like the heartbeat of a business,
indicating how efficiently it pumps revenue through its assets.

— Unknown

In today's consumer landscape, when faced with the need to make a purchase and explore available options, many individuals instinctively turn to Amazon for their shopping needs. What began as a humble online bookstore has now transformed into an unparalleled retail powerhouse, offering an extensive range of products spanning from toys and electronics to household essentials like hoses for central vacuum. Amazon's motto, "your margin is my lunch," encapsulates its relentless pursuit of market share and customer satisfaction. While the company's profit margin may appear modest, it compensates by capitalizing on the rapid turnover of its vast inventory, resulting in a remarkably high asset turnover.

This astute strategy has not gone unnoticed by investors, as Amazon's stock value has skyrocketed nearly tenfold over the past decade.

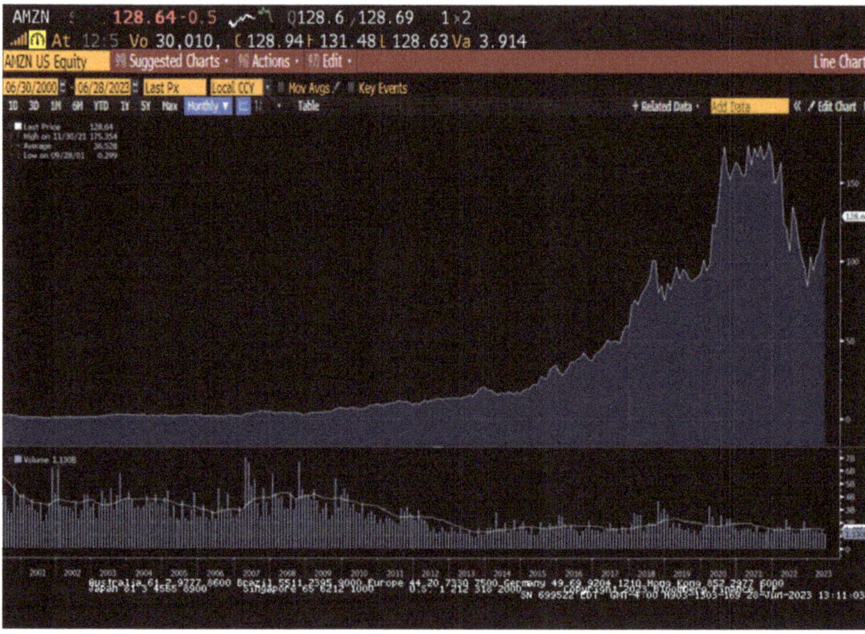

The company's success is underpinned by its ability to continuously meet the evolving demands and expectations of consumers, thereby solidifying its dominant position in the retail industry. Amazon's relentless focus on customer satisfaction, vast product selection, and innovative services has solidified its position as a go-to destination for consumers and a formidable force in the retail and technology sectors. Amazon's ability to continuously evolve, and invest in cutting-edge technologies in order to speed up its turnover of assets and meet the ever-changing needs of its vast customer base has cemented its status as a global leader and a true trailblazer in the world of e-commerce.

Amazon has undeniably disrupted numerous brick-and-mortar business models, leaving companies like Sears and Lord and Taylor as casualties of their failure to adapt to the advancements in technology. However, amidst this transformation, there is one notable exception: Walmart. As a multinational retail corporation, Walmart has managed to navigate the changing landscape with remarkable success. Renowned for its streamlined inventory management and impressive sales volume, the company has leveraged its extensive network of stores and robust supply chain capabilities to effectively convert its assets into revenue. By optimizing inventory management practices and harnessing the potential of its physical locations, Walmart has achieved a remarkable pace of asset turnover, capitalizing on its inventory and property to generate substantial income. This strategic approach has played a pivotal role in Walmart's ability to thrive in an era where many traditional retailers have faltered.

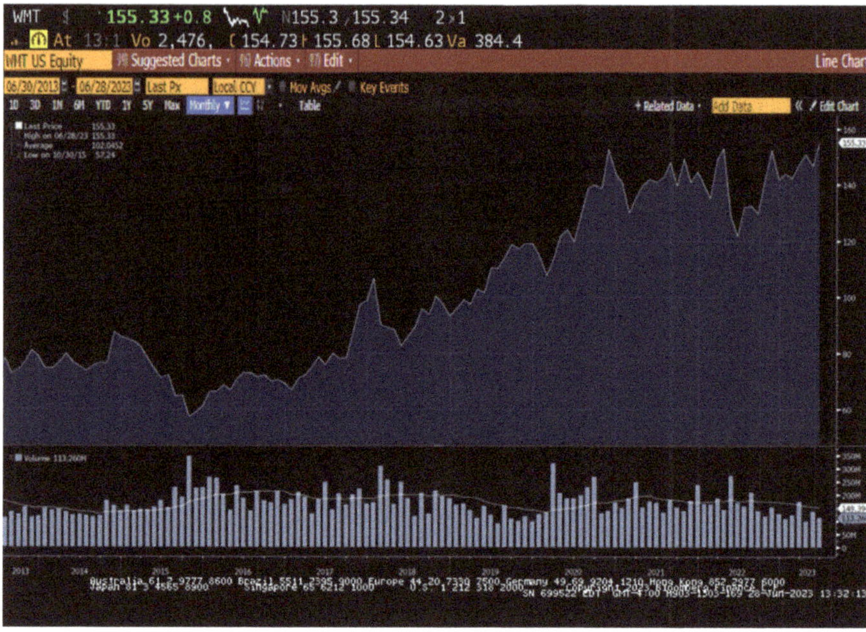

Asset Turnover is a vital metric that evaluates the management's ability to effectively utilize the company's assets in generating revenue. By dividing the revenue by the total assets, this ratio provides insights into the efficiency of asset utilization. When formulating a corporate strategy, it becomes crucial to assess different segments of the company and determine if certain lines of business and the assets within those businesses have reached a state of maturity with limited growth prospects.

Management should proactively estimate the return on its major assets and evaluate their significance to the company's overall success. By doing so, they can assess whether it would be advantageous for the company to discontinue the operations, sell the unit, or spin it off into a separate entity.

This strategic evaluation enables management to optimize the allocation of resources and focus on core areas that drive growth and profitability. By divesting non-essential assets, the company can streamline its operations, reduce potential risks, and unlock additional value for shareholders. Therefore, an effective strategy should perform a thorough assessment of asset performance and alignment with the company's objectives for maximizing shareholder value and ensuring long-term success.

Chapter 11
Leverage and Capital Structure

When you combine ignorance and leverage,
you get some pretty interesting results.

—Warren Buffett

Let us recall that, ultimately, the primary objective of the corporate strategy of a for-profit public company is to create value for its shareholders. A tangible and widely used measure of this value creation is the return on equity (ROE), which captures the profitability of the firm relative to the capital invested by its equity holders.

The fundamental source of this return is the firm's ability to produce goods and services that customers are willing to pay for. These goods and services are generated through a combination of human capital—namely, the skills, effort, and knowledge of the company's employees—and physical and intangible assets, such as machinery, information systems, transportation equipment, patents, and brand capital. Together, these inputs constitute the productive capacity of the firm.

Management's effectiveness in deploying these assets to generate revenues and operating profits is commonly measured by the return on assets (ROA). ROA reflects how efficiently the firm uses its asset base, independent of how those assets are financed, and therefore serves as an indicator of operational performance and managerial efficiency.

However, assets do not exist in isolation; they must be financed. The two primary sources of financing are debt and equity, each carrying its own risk profile and corresponding return demanded by capital providers. Debt holders require interest payments as compensation for relatively lower risk, while equity holders demand a higher expected return to compensate for residual risk. The proportion of debt relative to equity is referred to as the firm's financial leverage, and it plays a central role in shaping the relationship between ROA and ROE.

The overall cost of financing the firm's assets is summarized by the weighted average cost of capital (WACC), which represents the weighted average of the returns required by debt holders and equity holders, adjusted for their respective shares in the capital structure and, in the case of debt, the tax shield provided by interest deductibility. From a strategic perspective, value is created when the firm earns returns on its assets that exceed its WACC.

A commonly used simplified approach to estimating a firm's WACC begins by approximating the cost of debt and the cost of equity separately and then combining them according to the firm's capital structure.

The cost of debt is often approximated by the yield to maturity on the company's long-term debt, or, if that is not directly observable, by the yield on bonds with similar credit risk and maturity. This yield reflects the return required by debt holders, given the firm's default risk. Because interest payments are generally tax-deductible, the after-tax cost of debt used in WACC calculations is the pre-tax yield multiplied by (1 − tax rate).

Estimating the cost of equity is less straightforward, since equity does not have a contractual return. A standard approach is based on the Capital Asset Pricing Model (CAPM), which relates the expected return on equity to the systematic risk of the firm's stock. In its simplest form, this approach uses the stock's beta as a measure of its sensitivity to market movements and multiplies it by the long-term expected excess return of the stock market. In practice, this is often expressed as:

$$\text{Cost of Equity} = R_f + \beta \times (E[R_m] - R_f)$$

where R_f is the risk-free rate and $E[R_m] - R_f$ is the market risk premium. In the United States, the long-term historical average return of the S&P 500 has been approximately in the range of 11% to 12.5% per year, although the relevant input for CAPM is the excess return over the risk-free rate rather than the total market return.

Once the cost of debt and the cost of equity are estimated, WACC is calculated by weighting each component by its share in the firm's capital structure:

$$\text{WACC} = D/(D+E)r_d(1-T) + E/(D+E)r_e$$

where D and E denote the market values of debt and equity, r_d is the cost of debt, r_e is the cost of equity, and T is the corporate tax rate.

This approach yields an approximate value of WACC that is often sufficient for strategic analysis, capital budgeting, and valuation exercises. However, it is important to recognize that WACC is sensitive to assumptions about market returns, beta estimation, tax rates, and capital structure, and therefore should be interpreted as an estimate rather than a precise observable quantity.

After generating revenue from sales, the firm subtracts operating expenses, depreciation and amortization, interest payments on debt, and taxes. What remains is net income attributable to equity holders. Return on equity is therefore determined by the level of these residual earnings relative to the equity base, or equivalently, the number of shares outstanding. In this way, ROE reflects the combined effects of operating performance (ROA), financial leverage, and the cost of capital—linking corporate strategy, operational efficiency, and financial structure into a coherent framework for evaluating shareholder value creation.

By construction, ROA does not depend on the firm's capital structure—that is, on whether assets are financed by debt or equity. ROA is intended to capture the efficiency with which management deploys the company's asset base to produce goods and services and generate operating profits. As such, it reflects operating performance and managerial effectiveness rather than financing choices.

In contrast, ROE is directly influenced by the firm's financing decisions. ROE depends not only on operating profitability but also on the amount of interest paid on outstanding debt and on the number of shares outstanding. Financial leverage therefore, plays a central role in shaping ROE. Holding operating performance constant, changes in leverage can materially alter the returns earned by equity holders.

When the after-tax cost of debt is significantly lower than the firm's return on assets—or, equivalently, when the firm earns returns on its investments in excess of the cost of debt—an increase in leverage can enhance ROE. In such circumstances, a strategic approach to improving ROE may involve increasing the firm's debt and using the proceeds to repurchase shares. By reducing the number of shares outstanding, future earnings are spread over a smaller equity base, mechanically increasing earnings per share and ROE.

Share repurchases are often viewed as a more efficient mechanism for creating shareholder value than increasing dividends. Buybacks tend to support or increase share prices by reducing supply and signaling management's confidence in the firm's prospects, effectively putting a floor under the stock price. Moreover, from a tax perspective, share repurchases can be advantageous for equity holders: capital gains taxes on price appreciation are deferred until shares are sold, whereas dividends are typically taxed immediately upon receipt.

For example, in 2013, Apple Inc. made a significant move by announcing a $17 billion debt offering, marking its first debt issuance in over 17 years. This strategic borrowing was specifically aimed at funding its share repurchase program, which had the primary objective of returning capital to shareholders. By opting for a share repurchase program, Apple sought to create value for its shareholders in a tax-efficient manner.

Moreover, Apple's strong balance sheet and financial position played a crucial role in mitigating any potential risks associated with the debt issuance. Given the company's robust financial standing, adding debt to its capital structure did not significantly raise the overall risk level. Apple's ability to manage and service the debt, combined with its ample cash reserves, ensured that the borrowing did not compromise its financial stability.

In a share repurchase, the company buys back its own shares, thus reducing the total number of shares outstanding. This reduction, in turn, can lead to an increase in the share price, resulting in capital gains for shareholders when they eventually sell their shares. The advantage here is that shareholders can defer the payment of capital gains tax until they decide to sell their shares, potentially benefiting from a lower tax rate on capital gains compared to ordinary income.

By returning capital to shareholders through buybacks, Apple was able to provide a tax-efficient means for shareholders to realize value from their investments.

IBM, another prominent technology company, has also used debt to finance share buybacks as part of its capital allocation strategy. While the company regularly returns capital to investors through dividends, it made a noteworthy move in 2017 by issuing $4.5 billion in bonds specifically to support its share repurchase program.

Another way that a company can return capital to its investors is through dividends. Dividends represent a portion of the company's earnings that are distributed directly to shareholders on a per-share basis. While dividends are viewed as income and are taxed at the individual's income tax rate, capital gains are generally taxed at a lower rate in the United States.

A natural question that arises is whether the value of a firm depends on its capital structure and, relatedly, whether there exists an "optimal" capital structure that corporate strategy should seek to achieve. In other words, what is the appropriate mix of debt and equity used to finance the firm's assets, and does this mix have a material impact on the firm's valuation?

Debt financing involves borrowing funds from external sources, such as banks or bondholders, with a contractual obligation to make interest and principal payments. Equity financing, in contrast, involves raising capital through the issuance of ownership claims in the form of common or preferred shares, which do not require fixed payments but entitle shareholders to residual cash flows and control rights.

Debt financing offers several potential advantages. Most notably, interest payments on debt are typically tax-deductible, creating a tax shield that lowers the effective cost of capital. In addition, because debt holders bear less risk than equity holders, the cost of debt is generally lower than the cost of equity. These features imply that, up to a point, the use of debt can reduce the firm's WACC and increase firm value. However, excessive reliance on debt increases fixed financial obligations, heightens the risk of financial distress, and may impose restrictive covenants that limit managerial flexibility and future borrowing capacity.

Equity financing, on the other hand, provides a buffer against losses and enhances financial resilience. A larger equity base reduces the probability of default and allows the firm to better withstand economic downturns and unexpected shocks. Equity financing also avoids mandatory interest payments, thereby preserving cash flow during periods of weak performance. However, issuing additional equity dilutes existing shareholders' ownership and earnings per share, and may weaken managerial discipline by reducing the pressure imposed by fixed debt obligations. Moreover, equity is typically more expensive than debt, reflecting its residual claim on the firm's cash flows.

Modigliani–Miller have shown that under certain idealized assumptions, the capital structure of a firm does not affect its overall value and this proposition earned Modigliani and Miller the Nobel Prize in Economics in 1985.

The Modigliani–Miller theorem suggests that in a perfect world with no taxes, no transaction costs, perfect information, and efficient capital markets, investors can effectively create the capital structure they desire through financial engineering. This means that they can replicate any desired mix of debt and equity on their own, without relying on the company's capital structure decisions. Therefore, the company's choice between debt and equity financing would not impact its overall value. The theory argues that investors are primarily concerned with the company's underlying business and its expected cash flows rather than the specific mix of debt and equity used to finance those operations. In other words, as long as the cash flows remain the same, altering the capital structure will not change the total value of the company.

However, it is essential to recognize that the Modigliani–Miller theorem rests on several assumptions that may not hold in the real world. Factors such as taxes, bankruptcy costs, agency problems, and information asymmetry can influence the way capital structure decisions impact a company's valuation. In practice, these real-world frictions introduce complexities that can make the Modigliani–Miller theorem less directly applicable.

The trade-off between the benefits of debt—such as tax shields and lower financing costs—and the costs associated with financial distress, agency problems, and loss of flexibility lies at the heart of capital structure decisions. Corporate strategy must therefore balance these competing considerations when determining the firm's financing mix. The concept of an optimal capital structure emerges from this trade-off: a level of leverage at which firm value is maximized and WACC is minimized, given the firm's business risk, growth opportunities, asset characteristics, and operating environment.

In this sense, capital structure is not merely a financing choice but a strategic decision that can materially influence firm valuation, risk, and long-term value creation. That said, while leverage and share buybacks can enhance ROE and shareholder value under favorable conditions, they also increase financial risk. Higher debt levels raise fixed obligations and reduce financial flexibility, particularly during economic downturns. Consequently, decisions regarding leverage and capital return policies must be evaluated carefully within the broader context of risk, sustainability, and long-term value creation.

Chapter 12

Corporate Strategy: Evaluation and Implementation

Efficiency is doing things right; effectiveness is doing the right things.

— Peter Drucker

In this chapter, we discuss how the framework developed in the previous chapter—centered around the following formula—can be used both to devise a corporate strategy or to evaluate the effectiveness of one.

We begin by distinguishing between two types of companies: established firms with revenue and startups with no customers or revenue. For startups, a key strategic decision is how to fund operations during the early stages. For revenue-generating companies, the first step in strategic planning is to assess the company's position relative to its peers in the same industry.

This is done by bench marking the company's financial ratios against the mean and standard deviation of those same ratios within the peer group. Take, for example, the interest burden ratio, defined as EBT/EBIT. By comparing the company's ratio to the peer group average and measuring how many standard deviations it deviates from the mean, one can determine whether the company is an outlier.

A very low interest burden ratio suggests that the company faces a high interest expense and is likely over-leveraged, with a significant portion of its assets financed by debt. Conversely, a very high ratio may indicate that the company is under-leveraged and could potentially enhance its return on equity (ROE) by introducing more financial leverage.

It's important to go beyond evaluating individual ratios in isolation. Anomalies often become more evident when ratios are examined in pairs or triplets. For instance, a company may not appear to be an outlier when each metric is viewed separately, but it may stand apart from its peers when two ratios—such as (EBT/EBIT) and (EBITDA/Gross Profit)—are analyzed together. This concept is illustrated in the following hypothetical diagram.

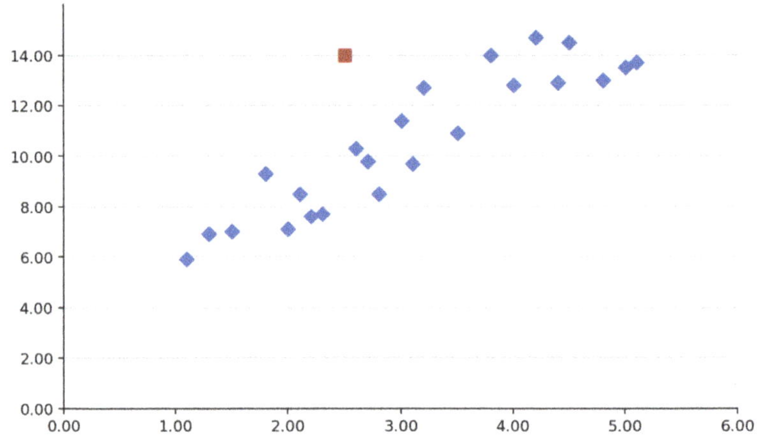

Since the primary objective of corporate strategy should be to create value for the firm's investors, which includes both lenders and equity shareholders, the corporate strategy should indicate its impact on ROE—a key metric that reflects the firm's ability to generate returns for equity investors. ROE can be decomposed into the product of various performance drivers shown above, therefore, management should analyze how the strategy influences each component of this formula.

It is important to recognize that strategy may affect different elements of the ROE equation in uneven or even opposing ways. What ultimately matters is the net effect on overall ROE and, by extension, shareholder value.

For example, suppose a key element of the firm's strategy is to enter a new market. This move might result in an increase in revenue due to expansion and access to new customers. At the same time, however, it could also lead to higher operating expenses, such as costs associated with marketing, logistics, or establishing a local presence. As a result, the (EBITDA/Gross

Profit) ratio (a measure of operating efficiency) might decline temporarily due to elevated overhead.

On the other hand, if the firm is able to sell higher-margin products or services in this new market, the (Gross Profit/Revenue ratio) could improve. That is, each dollar of revenue may now yield more gross profit than before. If the combined effect of these changes leads to an increase in the product of:

$$(\text{EBITDA/Gross Profit}) \times (\text{Gross Profit/Revenue}),$$

then the strategy can be considered effective—even if one component deteriorates—because the overall contribution to profitability has improved.

Therefore, a sound corporate strategy does not need to improve all metrics simultaneously. What matters is whether the strategy, as a whole, enhances the firm's ability to generate returns for its investors.

In addition to setting a strategy, management must actively monitor its implementation to ensure that it stays on track and make adjustments as needed. Profit—and therefore ROE—is ultimately a function of both revenue and expenses. Revenue is largely influenced by external factors such as market demand, customer preferences, and the competitive landscape. Although management can attempt to boost revenue through strategic actions—such as setting competitive prices, improving product quality, enhancing customer service, or entering new markets—ultimately, revenue generation is shaped by the behavior of customers and the dynamics of the broader market. In other words, while management can influence revenue, it cannot directly control it.

In contrast, expenses—or internal costs—are largely within the direct control of management. These include decisions around labor, procurement, operations, production processes, marketing budgets, and overhead. Effective cost management, therefore, plays a critical role in driving profitability and improving ROE. Strategic choices about where and how to allocate resources, which processes to streamline, and where to invest in automation or efficiency improvements can have a direct and measurable impact on net income.

Therefore, while revenue depends on the market, cost management is where corporate strategy can assert the most direct influence. A well-formulated strategy focuses not only on capturing value from the marketplace but also on preserving and enhancing that value internally through disciplined financial and operational management.

Financial Statements—including the Balance Sheet, Income Statement, and Statement of Cash Flows—are prepared primarily for external users, such as investors, creditors, and regulators. Their purpose is to provide a clear picture of the company's financial health, performance, and profitability over a given period. These statements help stakeholders evaluate the company's ability to generate earnings, manage assets and liabilities, and sustain long-term growth.

On the other hand, managerial accounting is designed for internal use by management. Its primary role is to support decision-making by providing detailed, timely, and relevant information about the company's cost structure, operations, and resource utilization. Managerial accounting focuses on understanding how costs behave in relation to various business activities—such as production volume, labor inputs, or marketing efforts—and how these costs impact overall performance.

It also plays a critical role in planning, forecasting, and budgeting. Through tools such as cost analysis, variance analysis, break-even analysis, and performance metrics, managerial accounting enables managers to:

- Plan and allocate resources more effectively
- Monitor operational efficiency
- Adjust strategies in response to actual performance and
- Align day-to-day decisions with broader strategic objectives.

In this way, managerial accounting serves as a vital feedback mechanism, helping organizations track the progress of their strategic initiatives, identify potential inefficiencies, and make informed decisions to improve outcomes. While financial accounting looks at the past to inform outsiders, managerial accounting looks to the future to help insiders make better choices.

One approach to cost monitoring and management is to determine the relationship between cost and production. A useful tool is using simple linear regression where

$$\text{Cost} = \alpha + \beta \text{ Production}$$

α can be viewed as the fixed cost and β as the variable cost. To estimate α and β historical data should be collected e.g., quarterly production (P_i) and costs (C_i) $i = 1, 2, \ldots, n$ are collected and α and β are selected such that sum of squared errors (SSE) is minimized

$$\text{SSE} = \sum (C_i - \alpha - \beta P_i)^2$$

Let C be the average quarterly cost $C = \sum C_i/n$ and $P = \sum P_i/n$ the average quarterly production

The total variability of cost is measured by $\text{TC} = \sum (C_i - C)^2$ similarly the total variability of production is measured by $\text{TP} = \sum (P_i - P)^2$.

The total variability of cost if it followed the model i.e., sum of squares due to regression is

$$\text{SSreg} = \sum (C - \alpha - \beta\ P_i)^2$$

It can be shown that TSS = SSreg + SSE.

The predictive power of the model is measured by R^2 = SSreg/TSS ≤ 1.

Let $\sigma = \sqrt{}(\text{SSE}/n)$.

Given production level of P^*, the predicted cost is $\alpha + \beta P^*$ with a standard deviation of $\sigma^* = \sigma 1/n + (P^* - P)^2/\text{TP}]$. This standard deviation can be used to determine if deviation of actual cost C^* from the predicted cost $\alpha + \beta P^*$ is significant and if so what is the root cause of it. In general a deviation exceeding $2\sigma^*$ should be deemed significant.

The function LINEST in EXCEL can be used to accomplish the above.

If a strategic plan requires an initial cash outlay—such as costs related to layoffs or entering a new market with the expectation of higher future profits—management should estimate how long it will take for the additional profits to offset that initial investment. This is commonly referred to as the break-even time.

A more precise approach is to discount the expected future profits at the company's cost of fund and calculate how long it takes for the discounted cash flows to equal the upfront expenditure. One way to estimate the cost of fund is to use the yield on the company's long-term debt at the time the investment is made. This yield has two components:

(i) The risk-free rate, typically represented by the yield on U.S. Treasury securities with similar maturities and
(ii) The credit spread, which reflects the company's credit risk and represents the additional return required by lenders to compensate for that risk.

Another important aspect of strategic planning is managing interest expense. Companies typically borrow at either a fixed rate, where the interest rate of the borrowing remains constant over the life of the loan, or a floating rate, which is periodically reset based on a benchmark index (e.g., monthly or quarterly).

If a company has borrowed at a fixed rate, and management anticipates that interest rates will decline, it can effectively convert its fixed-rate debt into floating-rate debt by entering into an interest rate swap. In this arrangement, the company agrees to pay a floating rate and receive a fixed rate, thereby offsetting the fixed interest payments on its debt. The net result is that the company's exposure shifts from fixed to floating, allowing it to benefit if market rates fall.

Conversely, if a company has floating-rate debt and is concerned that interest rates may rise—thus increasing the cost of servicing its debt—it can enter into a pay-fixed, receive-floating interest rate swap. This effectively locks in a fixed borrowing cost, providing protection against rising rates.

Beyond basic swaps, there are more innovative tools available for interest rate risk management. For example:

- **Interest rate caps**: These set an upper limit on the floating rate the company will pay, providing protection against rate spikes while allowing it to benefit from rate declines,
- **Zero-cost collars**: These combine a cap and a floor, offering downside protection while giving up some of the upside, often with no upfront premium.

These and other strategics are covered in greater detail in courses or texts on Financial Engineering, which provide a comprehensive toolkit for managing financial risks while optimizing capital structure.

Some strategic plans involve a company entering new activities or business lines. It's important to understand that such ventures often exhibit growth patterns that follow an S-curve, a common shape used to describe the life cycle of innovations, products, or market expansions. The S-curve typically includes three phases:

(i) **Initial Phase**: Slow growth due to early development, market uncertainty, and initial barriers.

(ii) **Acceleration Phase**: Rapid adoption and expansion as the offering gains market traction.
(iii) **Maturity Phase**: Growth slows and flattens as the market saturates or competition increases.

Understanding where a business is on this curve helps management make informed decisions about timing investments, reallocating resources, or pivoting strategy.

A critical feature of the S-curve is the inflection point, where the growth rate shifts from increasing to decreasing. Identifying this point is essential because it can serve as an early warning sign that growth is slowing, which may affect investor sentiment and stock price.

Mathematical Models: Gompertz and Weibull Curves

Two common models used to estimate and fit S-curve patterns are the Gompertz and Weibull functions.

1. Gompertz Function: The Gompertz curve is asymmetric and often used to model biological growth, technology adoption, and diffusion of innovations.
Formula:

$$y(t) = a \exp(-b \exp(-ct))$$

where:

$y(t)$ = size or sales at time t
a = upper asymptote (maximum achievable size)
b = constants related to displacement and growth rate

2. Weibull Function: The Weibull curve is often used in reliability engineering and failure analysis but is also applicable to modeling time-to-adoption or time-to-market saturation.
Formula (CDF):

$$y(t) = a(1 - \exp(-t/\lambda)^k))$$

where

$y(t) =$ cumulative value at time t
$a =$ maximum potential
$\lambda =$ scale parameter (time stretch)
$k =$ shape parameter (controls curve's steepness)

For $k > 1$, the curve has an S-shape.

Here's a diagram comparing the shapes of the Gompertz and Weibull functions:

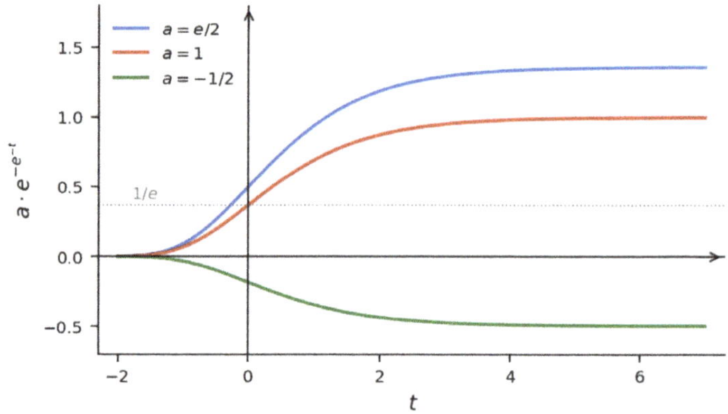

Gompertz Curve (a).

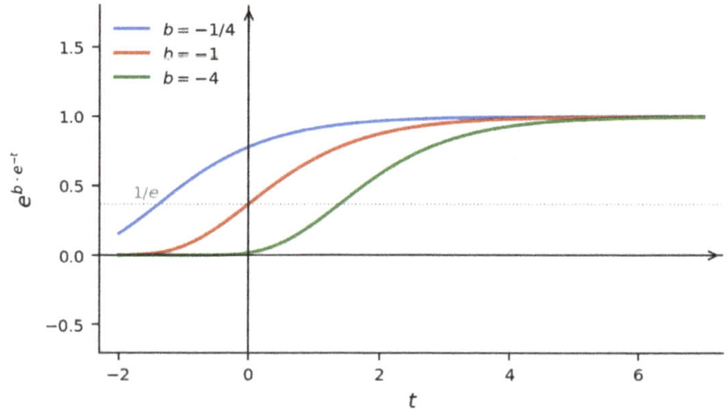

Gompertz Curve (b).

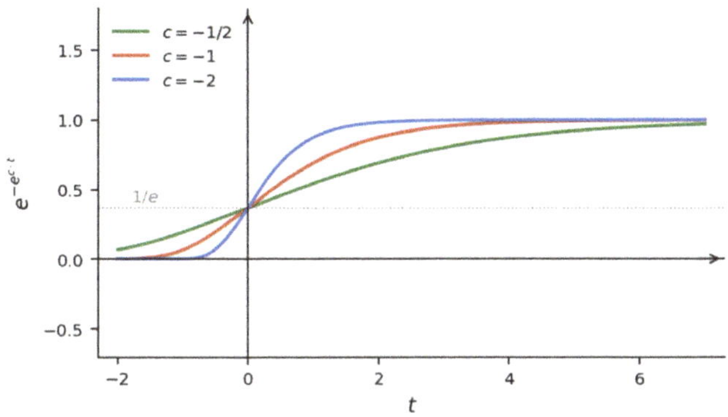

Gompertz (c).

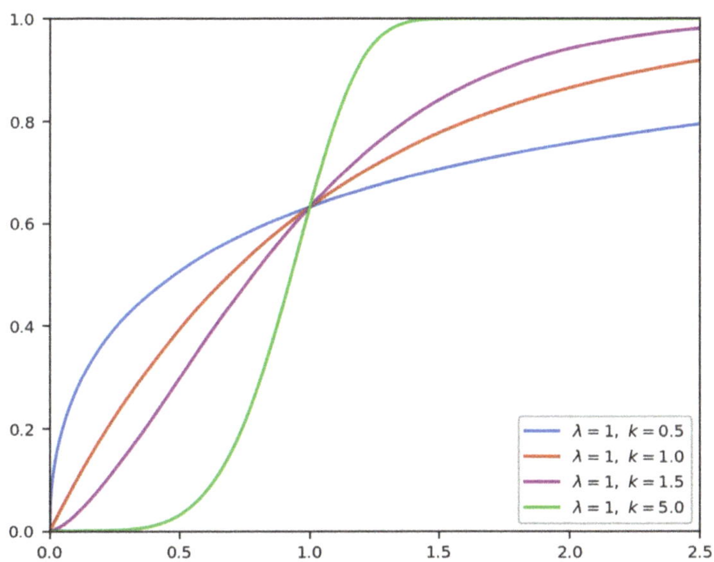

Weibull Curves

Application to Strategic Planning

By fitting actual or projected performance data to these models, companies can:

- Estimate time to inflection point
- Plan capital allocation more efficiently

- Time market entries or exit
- Forecast saturation levels

However, model accuracy depends heavily on data quality and contextual knowledge of the industry and market forces.

Another method that management can use for its forecasting of line of business with a trend is the use of Holt's two parameter family. This approach models the trend and level and at each step it adjusts its parameters α and β by smoothing them. Suppose the company has some initial sales number S_1, S_2, S_3, ... This approach needs and initialization of Level and Trend. There is no set rule since as the forecast progresses the impact of initialization starts to dissipate. One approach is to take the Initial level as the average of the first few observations, we take it to be say $L_0 = (S_1 + S_2)/2$. As for the trend we can follow a similar approach and let $T_0 = (S_3 - S_1)/2$. Having initialized the process the first forecast is $F_1 = L_0 + T_0$.

Now comes the updating scheme; Suppose we have predicted $F_n = L_{n-1} + T_{n-1}$ and S_n is the nth observation. We first update the level

$$L_n = (1 - \alpha)L_{n-1} + S_n$$

The trend is updated next

$$T_n = (1 - \beta)T_{n-1} + \beta(L_n - L_{n-1})$$

Now the forecast $F_{n+1} = L_n + T_n$

We have seen that the central objective of corporate strategy is to create shareholder value, which is commonly measured by the return on equity (ROE). ROE is a function of net income, which in turn is defined as:

$$\text{Net Income} = \text{Revenue} - \text{Expenses}$$

The case of startups with little or no revenue is fundamentally different from that of established companies, as many of the traditional performance metrics (e.g., ROE, interest burden, asset turnover) are not yet applicable. In these early stages, strategic decision-making is highly case-specific. For instance, the development path and challenges faced by a biotech startup working on a cancer drug differ significantly from those of a gaming startup. However, one common strategic element for both types of ventures is the question of how to fund operations—specifically, whether to raise capital through equity or convertible debt.

A crucial decision point arises when the startup needs funding to grow and transition to its next phase—for example, moving from product development to revenue generation. At this stage, the startup typically faces two primary funding options:

1. Equity Financing

Suppose an equity investor values the startup at X and is willing to invest αX in it. The post-money valuation of the company becomes:

$$X + \alpha X = X(1 + \alpha)$$

In this case, the current shareholders would give up:

$\alpha X/(X + \alpha X) = \alpha/(1 + \alpha) \times 100\%$ of the company to the new investor.

2. Convertible Debt Financing

Alternatively, the company may choose to raise the same amount, αX through convertible debt at an interest rate r, to be repaid or converted at a later date. The strategy here is to use this capital to grow the company over a time horizon t, at the end of which the company is expected to be worth βX.

Assuming the debt (including interest) converts into equity at that future valuation, the amount owed to the lender at that time (using continuous compounding for ease of calculations) will be $\alpha \mathrm{Xe}^{rt}$. The ownership stake that would be given up upon conversion is:

$$\alpha \mathrm{Xe}^{rt}/(\beta X + \alpha \mathrm{Xe}^{rt}) = \alpha/(\beta \mathrm{e}^{-rt} + \alpha)$$

To compare the two approaches, consider the condition under which both methods lead to the same dilution. This occurs when:

$$\alpha/(1+\alpha) = \alpha/(\beta \mathrm{e}^{-rt} + \alpha)$$

Solving for equality:

$$\beta \mathrm{e}^{-rt} = 1 \Rightarrow \beta = \mathrm{e}^{rt}$$

In other words, if the company's value grows at the same rate as the interest rate over time t, then equity financing and convertible debt result in equivalent dilution However, If the company's growth rate exceeds the interest rate (i.e., $\beta > \mathrm{e}^{rt}$), then debt financing is more advantageous for existing shareholders, as it results in less dilution. Conversely, if the interest rate exceeds the company's growth rate, equity financing is preferable, since the cost of servicing debt and converting it at a later stage would result in greater dilution.

Thus, in a low interest rate environment, convertible debt is typically the more attractive option. But in a high interest rate environment, especially if the company's growth potential is limited, equity financing may be the safer and more strategic choice.

Example:

Let's assume the following:

Initial company valuation: X =\$10 million
Funding required: αX=$0.5X$=\$5 million
Interest rate on convertible debt: $r = 10\%$
Investment horizon: $t = 2$ years

We will compare the percentage of ownership dilution under two scenarios:

(i) Equity financing at today's valuation
(ii) Convertible debt that converts into equity in 2 years, based on future valuation

Case 1: Equity Financing
Post-money valuation = $X+\alpha X$ = \$10 M+\$5 M=\$15 M

$$\text{Dilution} = 5/15 = 1/3 = 33.33\%$$

Case 2: Convertible Debt

Let's suppose the company grows to:

$\beta = 1.5$: Company grows 50% → Valuation becomes \$15 M
$\beta = 2$: Company doubles → Valuation becomes \$20 M
$\beta = 2.5$: Company grows 150% → Valuation becomes \$25 M

Amount owed at conversion (principal + interest compounded):

$$5\text{ M }(1+r)^t = 5\text{ M} \times (1.1)^2 = 5\text{ M} \times 1.21 = \$6.05\text{ M}$$

Now, the dilution is

$$\text{Dilution} = 6.05/(\beta \times 10)$$

Future Valuation βX	Dilution (%)
\$15 M ($\beta = 1.5$)	40.3
\$20 M ($\beta = 2$)	30.3
\$25 M ($\beta = 2.5$)	24.2

So, convertible debt is only better if the company's valuation increases more than 21% per year, i.e., if:

$$B > e^{rt} = e^{(0.1)\times 2} = e^{0.2} \approx 1.221$$

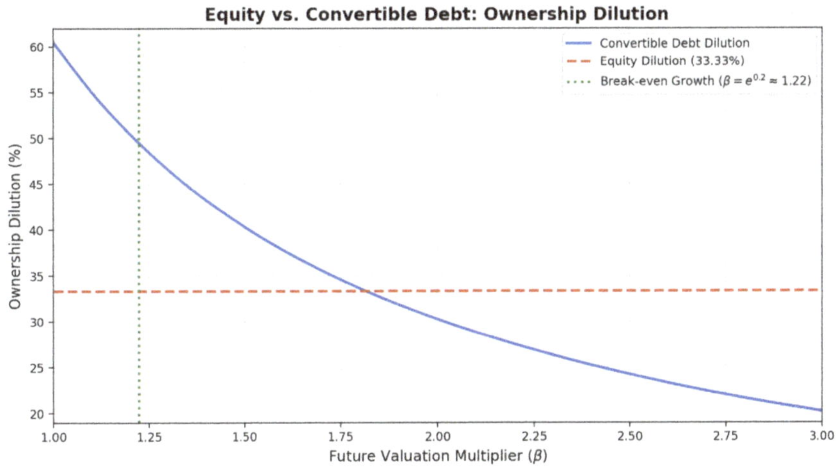

Equity vs. convertible debt: Ownership dilution.

Here is the graph comparing ownership dilution under equity financing versus convertible debt:

- The red dashed line shows dilution under equity financing, fixed at 33.33%.
- The blue curve represents dilution from convertible debt, which decreases as the future valuation (β\beta$\beta$) increases.

- The green dotted line marks the break-even point where both methods result in equal dilution—at around $\beta \approx 1.22$ (i.e., ~22% company growth over 2 years at a 10% interest rate). If the company expects to grow faster than ~22% over 2 years, convertible debt is the less dilutive option. If not, equity is safer.

Chapter 13

Prediction, Judgement, and Cognitive Biases

True Intuitive expertise is learned from prolonged experience
with good feedback on mistakes.

— Daniel Kahneman

As computational power continues to improve and its cost declines, the development of advanced Large Language Models (LLMs) such as ChatGPT, Gemini, Claude, and others is transforming the way managers access and use predictive analytics. These models now provide more frequent, nuanced, and context-sensitive predictions, enabling organizations to model a wider range of possible future scenarios—sometimes even attaching probabilities to their occurrence.

However, prediction alone is not sufficient for effective strategic decision-making. To formulate sound corporate strategies, predictions must be integrated with managerial judgment. This includes assessing the risks and potential rewards associated with each possible course of action. In this way, prediction and judgment are complementary: predictions offer insight into what might happen, while judgment determines what should be done in response.

Moreover, the role of judgment becomes even more critical when the forecasting horizon is long—such as in industries with extended product life cycles or capital-intensive investments. In these cases, the uncertainty surrounding predictions increases substantially, which diminishes the reliability of purely data-driven forecasts. Ironically, it is in precisely these high-uncertainty contexts where accurate prediction—if achievable—can be especially valuable, but also where human insight, experience, and strategic judgment become indispensable.

Ultimately, the interplay between algorithmic predictions and human judgment will define the future of strategic thinking. Managers must learn not just to consume predictions, but to critically evaluate and contextualize them within broader strategic frameworks.

Take, for instance, biopharmaceutical innovation. The long development timelines and highly uncertain outcomes associated with technological breakthroughs in this field make it nearly impossible to apply the conventional statistical models typically used for forecasting demand in consumer products. In such cases, firms must rely heavily on expert opinion and qualitative reasoning to assess critical factors and incorporate them into strategic planning.

These qualitative judgments often blend data with elements of extrapolation and imagination. However, caution is essential—extrapolation, especially in uncertain domains, can easily lead to misleading conclusions if not carefully grounded in realistic assumptions.

As managers are increasingly presented with a growing stream of model-based predictions, they must also be aware of the limitations of human cognition. As "boundedly rational" decision-makers, people are prone to blind spots, cognitive biases, and errors in judgment.

In this chapter, we explore the nature of managerial judgment, the common pitfalls and blind spots that can distort decision-making, and the methods by which managers can mitigate these limitations to make better strategic choices.

The time frame of the strategy is generally long-term, but the actual span of this horizon varies significantly across industries. For instance, in fast-evolving sectors such as software and information technology, "long-term" may refer to just three to five years, given the pace of innovation and disruption. In contrast, for capital-intensive industries like oil and gas, where infrastructure decisions and regulatory shifts unfold over decades, strategic horizons can stretch 20 years or more. For example, the ongoing transition toward lower carbon emissions requires oil companies to formulate strategies with multi-decade implications.

As the forecasting horizon extends, the reliability of quantitative models tends to diminish. Many traditional forecasting tools rely on historical data to identify patterns, but over long periods, the accumulation of error makes their predictions increasingly imprecise—interval estimates become so wide that they lose practical usefulness. More importantly, these models are inherently backward-looking: they are built on past observations and cannot account for factors or disruptions that have yet to emerge.

This limitation becomes especially problematic in the context of long-range strategic planning. Future technological shifts, regulatory changes, or entirely new business models may arise—many of which are not visible today. Some of the most critical variables that will shape the competitive environment 10 or 20 years from now may not even exist yet. Entire job categories, for example, may be created in the future that are unimaginable today.

In these circumstances, firms must turn to expert judgment and qualitative reasoning to bridge the gap. Identifying and incorporating such unknowns into strategic thinking requires more than data—it calls for imagination, scenario thinking, and informed extrapolation. These forecasts combine fragmentary data, expert intuition, and thoughtful anticipation of emerging trends. However, they must be approached with care. Extrapolation can easily lead to misleading conclusions if it extends beyond reasonable bounds or fails to account for structural shifts.

In short, when long-term strategic decisions are at stake, quantitative tools alone are insufficient. A balanced approach that integrates both data and judgment—anchored in rigorous reasoning but open to uncertainty and change—is essential for navigating an unpredictable future.

There is nothing inherently wrong with subjective forecasts—provided that management is fully aware of their limitations, especially the cognitive "blind spots" that can distort human judgment. When forecasts and scenario analyses are based on qualitative or subjective assessments, it is essential that decision-makers remain alert to behavioral biases that can skew these evaluations.

Below is a discussion of some of these biases followed by a brief explanation of the Delphi Method, which aims to reduce these kinds of distortions, along with its own potential shortcomings.

(I) Recency Bias: Recency bias occurs when individuals place disproportionate weight on recent events, especially those that are vivid or emotionally charged. This bias often leads to faulty extrapolations of short-term trends into the long-term future.

A striking example unfolded at the onset of the COVID-19 pandemic in early 2020. As the virus spread rapidly and lockdowns halted much of global movement, air travel experienced an unprecedented collapse. Investors, rattled by the scale and speed of the pandemic's impact, began comparing COVID-19 to HIV—another virus without a definitive cure—since both belong to the family of RNA viruses. This comparison, though superficial, led many to assume that COVID-19 would have similarly long-term, intractable consequences.

Under the influence of recency bias, investors concluded that air travel was entering a permanent decline. This sentiment led to widespread selling of airline stocks, sending prices into free fall. For instance, Southwest Airlines—a domestic carrier serving mainly medium-sized U.S. cities—saw its stock price plummet by about 50%. The following figure shows this dramatic drop.

South Wests' stock price decline.

The contagion of pessimism extended to airplane manufacturers as well. Boeing, a major supplier of commercial aircraft, saw its stock decline by roughly 54% during the same period.

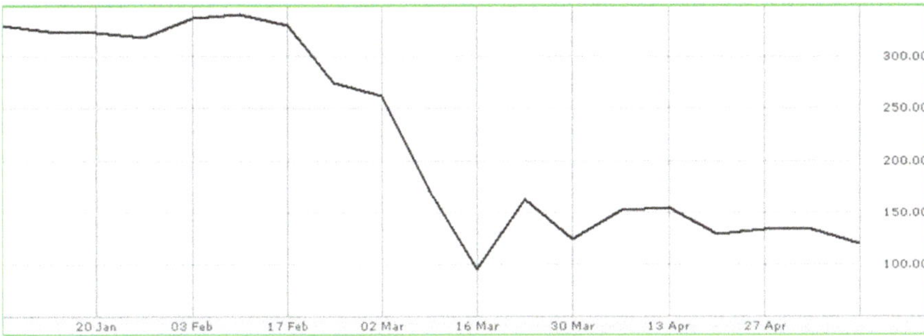

Boeing stock price decline.

Even Warren Buffett, the legendary value investor, sold off all of Berkshire Hathaway's airline holdings in May 2020. The fund reported a staggering loss for that quarter.

Yet these dire projections proved premature. The rapid development and roll-out of effective vaccines in late 2020 and 2021 reversed the trajectory of the pandemic and revived air travel. The earlier assumption that the industry was in permanent decline—largely driven by the emotional intensity and salience of recent events—turned out to be incorrect.

Recency bias also appears in other contexts. Marketing departments, for instance, sometimes project the success of a trending product far into the future, ignoring the cyclical nature of markets. One historical example is the telecommunications boom of the early 2000s. Companies like Global Crossing predicted skyrocketing demand for internet bandwidth and invested heavily in undersea fiber-optic cables. However, their linear extrapolations ignored broader economic fluctuations. The result: a massive oversupply of "dark fiber" (unused cable capacity) and the eventual bankruptcy of several firms.

In summary, recency bias can significantly impair forecasting and strategic decision-making. Managers must remain aware of how recent events can disproportionately shape perceptions and guard against overreacting to short-term fluctuations. Awareness of this cognitive pitfall—and tools to mitigate them—can help improve the quality of both subjective and data-driven forecasts.

(II) Availability Bias (a.k.a., Availability Heuristic): Another common cognitive blind spot is availability bias, where people rely on information that is most readily available or easily recalled from memory, rather than making the effort to gather more relevant or complete data. This tendency can lead to flawed conclusions, especially when individuals subconsciously seek out information that supports a preexisting belief—while ignoring or downplaying evidence that contradicts it.

As the saying goes, "You find what you're looking for." People often give more weight to vivid or memorable anecdotes, even when the supporting evidence is flimsy or anecdotal, and fail to consider broader data that might tell a different story.

A striking example is the 2003 invasion of Iraq, justified largely on the claim that Saddam Hussein possessed weapons of mass destruction (WMDs). Policymakers and intelligence agencies, driven by a predetermined narrative, selectively focused on fragments of information that appeared to support this assertion—while dismissing contradictory findings. This illustrates how availability bias, when combined with motivated reasoning, can lead to high-stakes misjudgments.

A more recent example can be seen in public resistance to COVID-19 vaccines during the 2020–2021 pandemic. Although adverse reactions to vaccines were extremely rare, media outlets often highlighted these exceptions to attract attention. These highly publicized cases became readily available in people's minds, leading some to believe—incorrectly—that the risks of vaccination outweighed its benefits. Rather than relying on large-scale data showing vaccine safety and effectiveness, many people based their judgment on isolated incidents, reinforcing vaccine hesitancy during a critical global health crisis.

(III) Anchoring Bias: Anchoring bias refers to the human tendency to rely too heavily on the first piece of information encountered—often called the "anchor"—when making decisions. In strategic planning, this bias can manifest when initial assertions or data points provided by management disproportionately influence subsequent thinking and decision-making.

For example, consider a situation in which management asserts that automation should be a key strategic initiative to improve market share or gross margins in certain product lines. While this might sound reasonable, such a statement can anchor the entire strategy development process around automation—leading teams to focus on justifying or executing that initiative rather than objectively evaluating a broader set of options. As a result, alternative paths that might be more effective or profitable could be overlooked.

Research has shown that anchoring bias can significantly impair rational investment decisions and erode economic value. In a notable study, scholars Zur Shapira and Myles Shaver conducted experiments showing that managers often reject decisions based on marginal profit analysis. This tendency leads them to undervalue potentially profitable investments that fall below historical averages, despite those investments generating positive returns.

The authors draw a compelling parallel to the leadership of Neville Isdell, former CEO of The Coca-Cola Company, who reportedly passed on a number of investment opportunities because they did not meet the company's historical profit margin of 30%. Anchored by this high-margin benchmark, Isdell rejected ventures that—while not as lucrative—could still have added value. In hindsight, these decisions reflected a costly adherence to an outdated anchor.

A similar pattern can be observed in the leadership transition at Microsoft. Steve Ballmer, the former CEO, placed strategic emphasis on high-margin areas such as video games. His strategic vision was anchored in profit margins rather than long-term innovation potential. When Satya Nadella took over as CEO, he shifted the company's focus toward cloud computing—a move that prioritized strategic relevance and future growth over short-term margins. This change in direction unlocked significant value and repositioned Microsoft as a leader in enterprise technology.

These examples underscore how anchoring bias, especially when tied to historical performance or early assumptions, can blind organizations to emerging opportunities and distort strategic judgment. Being aware of this bias is a critical step for managers to evaluate investments and strategies based on their forward-looking merits rather than outdated benchmarks or assumptions.

(IV) Selective Perception: Selective perception is a cognitive bias in which individuals interpret information through the lens of their prior experiences, beliefs, and expectations—often ignoring or downplaying data that challenges their assumptions. This bias becomes particularly problematic when managers project familiar frameworks onto unfamiliar contexts without critically examining whether the underlying conditions are comparable.

This tendency is especially common among executives transitioning from one industry to another. Leaders who have achieved success in a previous role may become overly confident in applying the same strategies in a new environment, even when the underlying dynamics differ significantly. Rather than adjusting their approach to fit the new context, they selectively perceive similarities and disregard critical differences.

For example, when John Sculley, a successful executive from PepsiCo, was appointed CEO of Apple Inc. in 1983, he brought with him a mindset shaped by the branded consumer goods industry. Although he had strong credentials in marketing and brand management, Sculley lacked experience in the fast-moving, innovation-driven world of high technology. He famously clashed with Steve Jobs and eventually ousted him from the company. Sculley then pursued a consumer branding strategy that proved ill-suited for a tech company whose competitive edge relied on product innovation and visionary leadership. Under his leadership, Apple stagnated and began to lose ground to its rivals.

The situation worsened with the appointment of subsequent CEOs who also failed to grasp the core innovation culture of Apple. Michael Spindler, primarily a marketing executive, and Gil Amelio, an operations-focused CEO with a background in engineering but little product vision, both failed to reverse the company's decline. These missteps reflected an ongoing pattern of executives applying frameworks that made sense in prior roles but not in Apple's context.

Another example is Harvey Golub, an accountant-turned-CEO of American Express. Golub's finance-heavy approach—focusing on numbers and accounting controls—limited his strategic vision and adaptability, ultimately leading to underperformance and leadership changes.

Selective perception narrows a manager's ability to adapt and make decisions based on a full and objective view of the situation. It encourages a kind of strategic tunnel vision, where past successes become templates for all future problems. This not only stifles innovation but can also lead companies into strategic dead ends.

To mitigate this bias, organizations must foster a culture of contextual awareness—encouraging leaders to question their assumptions, seek diverse viewpoints, and engage in rigorous analysis of the new environment before replicating past strategies. It also highlights the importance of industry-specific knowledge and adaptive learning in leadership transitions.

(V) Conservatism Bias: Conservatism bias refers to the tendency of decision-makers to cling to their existing beliefs or strategies even when presented with new, contradictory information. Ideally, strategic thinking should be adaptive—updating views and plans in light of new evidence. However, in practice, many managers update their beliefs much more slowly than what rational decision models would prescribe. This resistance to change can lead to strategic inertia and missed opportunities in dynamic markets.

A prominent example of this bias is found in the case of IBM's strategic missteps under former CEO Ginni Rometty. During her tenure, Rometty heavily emphasized Watson, the company's artificial intelligence (AI) platform, as the future growth engine for IBM—particularly targeting its application in the healthcare sector. Despite mounting evidence that Watson Health was under-performing, failing to deliver on its ambitious promises, and facing operational and technical challenges, Rometty remained committed to the strategy.

At the same time, the broader tech industry was rapidly pivoting toward cloud computing, with companies like Amazon (AWS), Microsoft (Azure), and Google investing heavily and gaining market share. Rather than aggressively pursuing cloud transformation early, IBM continued to allocate substantial resources to Watson—anchored in the belief that AI-driven healthcare would be a long-term differentiator.

Media and industry analysts repeatedly questioned IBM's strategy, pointing to declining revenues, missed innovation opportunities, and the company's eroding relevance in the broader tech landscape. Yet, management's course remained largely unchanged. Only after Rometty's departure did her successor, Arvind Krishna, shift IBM's focus decisively toward cloud computing and hybrid cloud infrastructure, including the spin-off of IBM's legacy managed services division and the acquisition of Red Hat to strengthen its position in the cloud market.

This case illustrates how conservatism bias can delay necessary strategic pivots, even in the face of clear signals from both the market and internal performance metrics. The costs of such inertia can be high—not just in missed growth opportunities, but also in reputational damage and organizational morale.

To overcome this bias, companies must foster a culture that values evidence-based decision-making and rewards strategic flexibility. Regular strategic reviews, feedback loops, and a willingness to challenge core assumptions are essential for avoiding the trap of sticking with outdated views in a changing world.

(VI) Illusory Correlation: Illusory correlation refers to the mistaken belief that a strong association between two variables implies a causal relationship. This bias arises when individuals observe two variables moving together and infer that one causes the other, without considering the possibility that the relationship may be coincidental or influenced by a third factor.

In strategy, this bias can be particularly dangerous. Managers may observe a statistically significant correlation and, without further scrutiny, base major strategic decisions on it—potentially leading to poor outcomes. It's important to remember that correlation does not imply causation, no matter how compelling the data may appear.

A classic example often cited in statistics classrooms involves the high correlation ($r = 0.96$) between per capita mozzarella cheese consumption and the number of civil engineering doctorates awarded in the United States between 2000 and 2009. While the data trends together impressively, there is clearly no logical or causal link between these variables. Despite the absurdity of such examples, similar reasoning errors occur in real-world decision-making, especially when decisions are made under pressure or when data is over-relied upon without context or critical analysis.

One noteworthy case of illusory correlation occurred in UK health policy. In 2016, a senior Tory politician claimed that "around 6,000 people lose their lives every year because we do not have a proper seven-day service in hospitals. You are 15 per cent more likely to die if you are admitted on a Sunday compared to being admitted on a Wednesday." The implication was that weekend staffing shortages in hospitals caused the elevated mortality rates.

While the correlation between day of admission and mortality rate did exist, the conclusion about causality was flawed. A more plausible explanation is that patients admitted on weekends tend to be in a more critical condition, as those with less urgent issues might wait until Monday. In other words, the higher mortality rate on Sundays may reflect differences in patient severity, not staffing levels. Unfortunately, such flawed reasoning can lead to misguided policy reforms, misallocation of resources, or erosion of public trust.

In strategic planning, the danger of illusory correlation lies in its seductive simplicity. Managers may see a pattern and conclude, for instance, that an increase in advertising spend directly causes higher sales—when in fact, both may be driven by an unobserved third variable such as seasonality or broader market trends.

To mitigate this risk, firms should:

- Use robust statistical techniques to test for causality (e.g., controlled experiments, Granger causality tests, regression with controls).
- Encourage cross-functional collaboration between data analysts and decision-makers to ensure proper interpretation of results.
- Avoid over-reliance on trend-based dashboards without investigating the underlying mechanisms.

Ultimately, while correlation can be a valuable signal, treating it as evidence of causality without rigorous analysis can lead to strategic missteps, faulty assumptions, and even reputational damage.

(VII) Framing Lock-ins: Framing lock-ins refer to the tendency of managers to interpret new situations using outdated mental models or conventional representations of their environment. These cognitive shortcuts—while helpful in reducing complexity—can become liabilities when environmental conditions change significantly. By continuing to view the world through the same old lens, managers risk making strategic decisions that are misaligned with new realities.

Mental models and simplified frameworks are essential tools for coping with information overload. They allow managers to quickly process complex inputs and reach decisions efficiently. However, when confronted with technological shifts, regulatory changes, or institutional disruptions, these once-useful frames can become strategic blinders. Persisting with outdated representations leads to what scholars call frame rigidity—the inability to re-frame problems or rethink underlying assumptions in light of new evidence.

A classic example of framing lock-in is Kodak's introduction of the Photo CD in the early 1990s. At the time, Kodak was facing increasing pressure from the digitization of photography and competitive threats from electronics firms such as Sony. In response, Kodak introduced the Photo CD, a digital storage device that allowed users to transfer and view photographs on compact discs.

This move, however, was heavily anchored in Kodak's traditional "razor-and-blade" business model—a strategy in which the core hardware is sold at low cost, with profits generated from the recurring sale of consumables. This model had long defined Kodak's success: consumers bought inexpensive cameras but had to continuously purchase film and pay for processing. The company hoped that the Photo CD would follow a similar pattern, where consumers would pay repeatedly to digitize and store their photos on CD-ROMs.

Yet, this framing missed the true nature of the digital revolution in photography. The real disruption was not merely the digitization of images, but the dematerialization of the entire photographic process—the shift from hardware- and consumable-dependent business models to software-centric, data-driven ecosystems. What Kodak failed to grasp was that in the digital world, the value chain was moving away from physical products (like film and CDs) and toward platforms, services, and instant sharing—domains where Kodak lacked expertise and vision.

In essence, Kodak's Photo CD was a digital product shackled to an analog-era business logic. Rather than rethinking the core assumptions about value creation in photography, Kodak tried to retrofit a new technology into an old frame—thereby missing the broader transformation that was underway. As a result, Kodak fell further behind while companies like Canon, Nikon, and eventually smartphone manufacturers capitalized on the real trends.

The lesson for strategic leaders is clear: when the external environment changes, so too must the internal cognitive frames through which decisions are made. Framing lock-ins can cause organizations to:

- Misinterpret the nature of disruption.
- Overinvest in legacy models that no longer deliver a competitive advantage.
- Miss opportunities for innovation and reinvention.

To guard against framing lock-ins, firms must foster a culture of critical reflection, external scanning, and diverse perspectives. Encouraging teams to challenge core assumptions, learn from failures, and update mental models in light of changing evidence is crucial for maintaining strategic agility.

(VIII) Loss Aversion: Loss aversion is a well-documented cognitive bias that describes how individuals tend to experience the pain of losses more intensely than the pleasure of equivalent gains. This concept was formalized by Daniel Kahneman and Amos Tversky in their groundbreaking Prospect Theory, which challenged traditional economic assumptions of rational decision-making.

Experiments consistently show that people are generally more motivated to avoid losses than to achieve gains. For example, psychologists have found that the distress caused by losing $50 is more intense than the satisfaction of gaining $50—so much so that a person who gains $100 but then loses $50 may feel worse than someone who simply gains $50. Despite the net gain being identical in both scenarios, the emotional weight of the loss dominates.

This asymmetry in how we evaluate outcomes has significant implications in strategic management, investment decisions, mergers and acquisitions, and corporate innovation. For instance, a management team may choose to forgo a high-upside strategic investment simply because the potential downside triggers a stronger emotional reaction—even if the expected value of the investment is clearly positive. As a result, companies can become overly cautious, risk-averse, and locked into the *status quo*.

A related consequence is that management may hold onto underperforming business units or projects longer than they should, simply to avoid the psychological discomfort of admitting a loss. This is often described as "throwing good money after bad," and it can result in sustained value destruction.

Inconsistency in Strategic Application: Another challenge related to cognitive biases in corporate strategy is inconsistency in how decision criteria are applied. Senior leaders often develop emotional attachments or "pet projects" and fail to subject them to the same rigorous evaluation applied to other initiatives. This inconsistency can lead to misallocation of capital, internal resentment, and the pursuit of strategically unjustified ventures. When strategic filters are not uniformly applied, the overall coherence and integrity of the firm's strategy are undermined.

Optimism Bias and Wishful Thinking: Optimism bias—another common cognitive distortion—manifests when management overestimates the likelihood of positive outcomes and underestimates potential obstacles. Following strategic planning sessions, executives often emerge with a euphoric sense of achievement and prematurely declare success before any implementation or results have materialized. This can result in a temporary boost in stock price, media accolades, or employee enthusiasm—only to be followed by disappointment when actual outcomes fall short of projections.

Examples abound in corporate history. Consider the case of Robert Allen, former CEO of AT&T, who led the company into the credit card business, rationalizing the move by pointing to AT&T's low funding costs. The initiative, however, ignored AT&T's lack of experience in consumer finance and ultimately failed. Similarly, Michael Armstrong, another AT&T CEO, pursued multiple spin-offs that were poorly executed and misaligned with market dynamics, leading to disappointing results.

Attribution Bias

Finally, strategic leaders should be wary of attribution bias—the tendency to credit success to internal factors such as managerial skill or vision, while blaming failures on external factors like market volatility, regulation, or "bad luck." This bias hampers organizational learning and prevents the honest postmortem necessary to improve future decision-making. When victories are seen as proof of brilliance and failures dismissed as flukes, organizations fail to build the introspective culture required for long-term resilience.

In conclusion, Loss aversion, optimism bias, inconsistency, and attribution error are just a few of the cognitive traps that strategic leaders must navigate. Being aware of these biases is the first step; creating deliberate processes, diverse decision-making teams, and checks and balances is essential to mitigate their influence. Strategy is as much about avoiding false confidence and faulty reasoning as it is about bold vision and execution.

One Way to Deal with Cognitive Biases: The Delphi Method

When management is confronted with subjective forecasts, strategic assertions, or uncertain scenarios—particularly in areas involving high ambiguity or limited historical data—cognitive biases can distort judgment and decision-making. One effective way to reduce such biases and synthesize diverse expert opinions is the Delphi Method, developed in the 1950s by the RAND Corporation. Originally created to explore future threats to U.S. national security during the Cold War, the Delphi Method has since been widely adopted in fields such as technology forecasting, public policy, and corporate strategy.

The Delphi Method is an iterative, anonymous, and structured process for gathering expert opinions and reaching convergence through successive rounds of feedback. Here's how it generally works:

- An initial set of questions—typically focused on a single issue or scenario (e.g., "What is the most significant threat to the long-term survival of this firm?")—is distributed to a panel of experts.
- Each expert responds independently and anonymously, which reduces the influence of dominant personalities or social pressures that can arise in group discussions.
- The responses are aggregated, analyzed, and then shared with the group, without attribution to individuals. Experts are encouraged to revise their earlier answers in light of the anonymized feedback from their peers.
- This process is repeated in multiple rounds until a consensus is reached or the range of answers stabilizes.
- The power of the Delphi Method lies in its ability to harness collective intelligence while mitigating groupthink, anchoring bias, and undue influence from authority figures.

To improve its effectiveness in a strategic setting, the Delphi Method can be combined with quantitative models or scenario planning tools, offering a more robust approach to forecasting and strategic risk analysis.

However, management should be aware of the method's limitations and design sensitivities. For example, when presented with Delphi results, it is important to ask:

- Who were the selected experts, and what criteria were used to identify and validate their expertise?
- How many experts participated in the process, and does the sample represent a range of perspectives?
- How many rounds of iteration were conducted, and did the responses converge naturally or under pressure?
- Was care taken to avoid social conformity or reputation bias—such as when a well-known expert is included and inadvertently sways others, even in an anonymous setting?
- Were the framing of questions and the interpretation of responses neutral and clearly defined?

The Delphi Method offers a disciplined framework to overcome some of the cognitive and social biases that plague strategic decision-making. When applied thoughtfully and transparently, it can provide valuable insight into complex, uncertain, and high-stakes decisions—especially when data alone are insufficient to chart a clear path forward.

Chapter 14

Black Swans: Preparing for Extreme Events

Rare events cannot be estimated from empirical observation since they are rare.

— Nassim Nicholas Taleb

The COVID-19 pandemic of 2020 and its dire economic consequences for a number of businesses showed once again the importance of rare events that have a major impact on the finances of a business. These impacts could be positive or negative. For example, during the pandemic, the cruise industry was badly hurt, and its revenue plunged to zero, and companies had to borrow money to survive. On the other hand, firms such as Zoom that were in the business of remote communications saw their fortune grow tremendously.

Carnival Cruise stock price.

Zoom Communications stock price.

Rare events with major and disproportional consequences are referred to as Black Swans—a term coined by Nassim Taleb. Such events create a daunting challenge for strategies that try to forecast their nature and the probability of them happening by using data or scenario analysis. The simple fact is that these events are rare hence there are no observed data and they can be quite varied. Some strategies use a number of possible and "reasonable" scenarios assign probabilities to them happening and try to "optimize" the decision and strategy based on these probabilities ignoring the fact that black swans are unkwown-unkwown events and trying to imagine them is a fool's errand. It is far more effective that rather than focusing on the nature of such events consider their impact, such as 30% fall in company's revenues or increase in sales by 50%.

For example, before the pandemic, Zoom was one of many video conferencing platforms, used primarily by corporate teams and tech-savvy users. It had steady but modest market penetration. The COVID-19 pandemic turned Zoom into a household name almost overnight. As remote work, online learning, and virtual socialization became the norm, Zoom's user base exploded. Daily meeting participants grew from 10 million in December 2019 to over 300 million by April 2020. Revenue for FY2021 increased by 326% year-over-year, and net income skyrocketed to $672 million, compared to just $21 million the year before.

Similarly, Peloton offered premium home fitness equipment combined with a subscription-based digital workout platform. Pre-pandemic, it was popular among affluent, urban customers. With gyms closed and people stuck at home, Peloton experienced a dramatic surge in demand. Revenue rose from $915 million in FY2019 to $4.0 billion in FY2021. Subscriptions more than tripled, and the company couldn't keep up with demand—wait times for bikes were several weeks. Peloton became a cultural symbol of high-end pandemic fitness.

On the other hand, Airlines were among the hardest-hit industries during the pandemic. They are capital-intensive, low-margin businesses that depend on high load factors and business travel. In 2020, global air traffic dropped by 60–70%. U.S. airlines lost over $35 billion in 2020 alone. Many routes were canceled, and international travel all but stopped. Business travel—which made up a disproportionate share of airline profits—collapsed.

When presented with a strategy by consultants, management should inquire about distributional assumptions used in the planning and whether these distributions have "thin tail" like normal distribution or "fat tail" that are a better model of rare events. The following are examples of using probability distribution in corporate strategy:

- A firm launching a new product with uncertain demand instead of predicting a single sales figure, it models demand as a probability distribution and estimates expected revenue, best/worst-case scenarios, and the likelihood of breaking even. This can help to determine how much inventory to produce, whether to outsource production, or how to price the product.
- A company evaluating whether to invest in a risky R&D project (e.g., a pharmaceutical firm evaluating a new drug) and use a probability distribution for project outcomes, such as time to completion, success probability, or payoff value and rather than a binary go/no-go decision, the firm evaluates a distribution of NPVs (Net Present Values).
- An airline wants to prepare for uncertain fuel prices or interest rate changes. It can model fuel price fluctuations using a lognormal or triangular distribution based on historical data and expert input and simulates profits or cash flows under various economic scenarios.
- A manufacturer needs to plan production under uncertain lead times or demand. It can model the lead times as Poisson or exponential distributions; demand as normal or discrete distribution the quantifying risk of stockouts vs. excess inventory. This can help in setting safety stock levels, supplier diversification, or flexible manufacturing capacity.
- A firm considers acquiring a competitor but faces uncertain synergies and integration costs. It uses probability models to estimate the distributions for cost savings, integration time, and revenue uplift and uses simulation instead of relying of a single DCF (Discounted Cash Flow) mode. This approach can help in determining offer price, structure of deal, or whether to walk away.
- A firm planning long-term workforce needs in light of retirement rates and turnover. It can mode attrition and retirement as binomial or Weibull distributions and estimate how quickly positions will open or which skills will become scarce. This can drive recruitment, training investment, or automation strategies.

- A tech startup deciding when to enter a new market with regulatory uncertainty. Regulatory approval timing can be modeled using a probability distribution (e.g., exponential) that allows estimation of NPV under different market-entry timing scenarios. This will help in the strategic decision of whether delay entry, partner with local firms, or invest in lobbying or legal strategy.

A mathematical discussion of Normal and other distributions and "Extreme Value" theory and power laws that deal with rare events is beyond the scope of this book however, the basic ideas can be discussed heuristically. Normal distribution is one of the widely used distributions in statistics. It has many desirable mathematical properties and can be shown that if observations have certain properties then the distribution of their average will tend towards normal. This fact is so central to many statistical and probabilistic techniques that it is called the Central Limit Theorem. This and many other distributions that are widely used to model the stochastic nature of events have what is called "thin tale" that implies the probability of rare events are very low according to these models. For example in the case of Normal distribution an event that is three standard deviations from the mean is supposed to happen less than once a century and when such models are used when the underlying process has "fat tail" people are surprised by the frequency of observing such events more frequently as evidenced by the recurrent market crashes.

For example, on October 19, 1987 the Dow Jones Industrial Average fell 22.6% in one day—the largest one-day percentage drop in U.S. stock market history. A single-day drop of that magnitude was unprecedented. Most financial models (especially those assuming a normal distribution of returns) gave virtually zero probability to such a drop. The crash erased hundreds of billions in market value globally and triggered panic selling. It shook confidence in computerized trading and market stability, leading to widespread regulatory changes (like circuit breakers). The crash revealed the fragility of systems built on flawed models, especially those underestimating tail risk.

The Credit Crisis of 2007–2008 was Triggered by widespread defaults on subprime mortgages in the U.S. and culminated in the failure of major financial institutions (e.g., Lehman Brothers), massive bailouts, and a global recession. The collapse of the modern financial system due to mortgage-backed securities was not widely anticipated. Risk models (like Value-at-Risk or Gaussian copulas) underestimated systemic interdependence and tail risk. Global GDP contracted; millions lost jobs and homes; stock markets lost trillions; central banks and governments had to coordinate unprecedented bailouts and stimulus packages. The crisis highlighted the danger of over-reliance on models that assume normality and independence.

One property of distributions with "thin tail" is that all the moments of these distributions, e.g., mean, standard deviation etc., exist, i.e., are finite. On the other hand a class of functions that have "fat tails" is power functions, and for these distributions some moments do not exist. For some power distributions even the first moment, that is, the mean in not finite. Another difference between these distributions and those with "thin tail" is their scalability. For illustration, consider the normal distribution and the probability of events greater than x, $2x$, and $4x$. For ease of calculation, let $x = 1$. Let us consider the same events for the simple power function

$$f(x) = 1/x^2 \quad x \geq 1$$

that has "fat tail." In the case of the normal distribution this ratios quickly goes to zero, whereas in the case of power function it is almost constant. The practical implication of this is that for "thin tail" distributions the chance of two consecutive say unfortunate events of magnitude x is much higher than observing a disastrous event of magnitude $2x$, whereas in the case of the fat tail distribution, the chance of experiencing a disaster of magnitude $2x$ is not negligible compared to two events of magnitude x. And usually, such large magnitude events can put the company in distress.

In the case of such large magnitude events the so called black swans, the attempt to predict the nature of such events and their probability is not feasible. A more productive approach is for the strategy to have contingency plans for the impact of such events that are much easier to fathom than the very nature of them. For example, what should the company do if because of some rare events its revenue drops by more than 30% as was the case for a number of companies during the pandemic of 2020, for example Airlines and Cruise Companies. Or foreign sales drop by 20% because of new tariffs. Having a contingency plan for such events can go a long way in enabling the company to adapt itself to new environment relatively quickly and use this quick adaptation as a competitive advantage.

Another technique that can be used to estimate the time and the challenges in implementing a strategy is using simulation. And to account for Black Swan events that could derail implementation of a strategy, one could use power function in the simulation.

Chapter 15
Conclusion

A conclusion is simply the place
where you got tired of thinking.

— Dan Chaon

Corporate strategy plays a pivotal role in ensuring the long-term survival and growth of a firm. Its primary objective is to create value for shareholders by enhancing various fundamental elements discussed in previous chapters. By focusing on these quantifiable elements, management can achieve tangible improvements that are measurable and contribute to the overall success of the organization.

When formulating corporate strategy, it is crucial for management to be aware of and guard against the influence of human biases. Cognitive biases can distort decision-making and hinder the effectiveness of strategic plans. By actively recognizing and mitigating these biases, management can make more objective and rational choices, leading to more robust and successful strategies.

In addition to addressing biases, corporate strategy should encompass contingency plans to handle the potential impacts of Black Swan events. These unexpected and rare occurrences have the potential to disrupt businesses significantly. By integrating contingency plans into the strategic framework, companies can proactively prepare for such events, allowing for more rapid adaptation and minimizing the negative consequences. A well-designed contingency plan can provide a roadmap for navigating uncertainty, protecting the firm's interests, and enabling timely responses to unforeseen challenges.

Simulation serves as a valuable tool for management to study various outcomes and assess the likelihood of their occurrence. By simulating different scenarios, decision-makers can gain insights into the potential consequences of their strategic choices. Simulations provide a controlled environment to explore multiple possibilities, assess risks, and evaluate the effectiveness of different strategies. This helps management make informed decisions, identify potential pitfalls, and refine their strategic plans based on a deeper understanding of the potential outcomes.

In summary, corporate strategy is crucial for creating shareholder value and improving key elements of the organization. To ensure the effectiveness of the strategy, management must be mindful of human biases that can hinder decision-making. Furthermore, the strategy should incorporate contingency plans to address the impact of Black Swan events, thereby enhancing the firm's resilience. Finally, utilizing simulation allows management to explore various outcomes and their probabilities, empowering them to make informed choices and optimize their strategic plans. By integrating these considerations, companies can enhance their competitive position, adapt to changing circumstances, and drive sustainable growth.

Bibliography

1. Zvi Bodie, Alex Kane, and Alan J. Marcus. 2023. *Investments*. McGraw-Hill Education.
2. Stephen Ross, Randolph Westerfield, Jeffrey Jaffe, and Bradford Jordan. (2019). *Corporate Finance*: McGraw-Hill Education.
3. Frederick Hillier and Gerald Lieberman. 2021. *Introduction to Operations Research.* McGraw Hill.
4. Richard Brealey, Stewart Myers, and Franklin Allen. 2016. *Principles of Corporate Finance*. Mcgraw-hill/Irwin Series in Finance, Insurance, and Real Estate.
5. Aswath Damodaran. 2025. *Investment Valuation: Tools and Techniques for Determining the Value of Any Asset*. Wiley Finance.
6. Ruth Bender and Keith Ward. 2008. *Corporate Financial Strategy*. Routledge.
7. Spyros G. Makridakis, Steven C. Wheelwright, and Rob J. Hyndman. 1997. *Forecasting: Methods and Applications.* John Wiley & Sons Inc.
8. Nassim Nicholas Taleb. 2007. *The Black Swan: The Impact of the Highly Improbable.* Random House.
9. Daniel Kahneman, Paul Slovic, and Amos Tversky (Eds.). 1982. *Judgment Under Uncertainty: Heuristics and Biases.* Cambridge University Press.
10. Steve L. Allen. 2003. *Financial Risk Management: A Practitioner's Guide to Managing Market and Credit Risk.* Wiley.
11. Tage C. Tracy. 2024. *How to Read a Financial Report: Wringing Vital Signs Out of the Numbers.* Wiley.
12. Stephen Penman. 2012. *Financial Statement Analysis and Security Valuation.* McGraw-Hill Education.

13. Howard Schilit and Jeremy Perler. 2010. *Financial Shenanigans: How to Detect Accounting Gimmicks & Fraud in Financial Reports*. McGraw-Hill.
14. John Tennent and Graham Friend. 2005. *Guide to Business Modelling*. Bloomberg Press.
15. Bob Vause. 2015. Guide to Analyzing Companies. *The Economist*.
16. Sun Tzu and Dangello Medina. 2020. *The Art of War*. Independently Published.
17. Richard Rumelt. 2011. *Good Strategy, Bad Strategy: The Difference and Why it Matters*. Profile Books.

Index